THE

CHURCH OF SCOTLAND.

By the same Author.

Lectures on the History of the Jewish Church.

PART I. — Abraham to Samuel. With Maps and Plans. $2.50.

The Same.

PART II. — From Samuel to the Captivity. Each one volume crown 8vo, cloth, *new and cheaper edition.* $2.50.

Lectures on the History of the Eastern Church,

With an Introduction on the Study of Ecclesiastical History. One volume crown 8vo, cloth, *new and cheaper edition.* $2.50.

Sinai and Palestine.

One volume crown 8vo, cloth, *new and cheaper edition.* $2.50.

Sermons Preached before His Royal Highness the Prince of Wales,

During his Tour in the East, in the Spring of 1862. One volume 12mo, cloth. $1.50.

☞ *Sent postpaid, on receipt of price.*

LECTURES ON THE HISTORY

OF THE

CHURCH OF SCOTLAND,

DELIVERED IN EDINBURGH IN 1872.

BY

ARTHUR PENRHYN STANLEY, D. D.

DEAN OF WESTMINSTER,

CORRESPONDING MEMBER OF THE INSTITUTE OF FRANCE.

NEW YORK:
SCRIBNER, ARMSTRONG, AND COMPANY,
SUCCESSORS TO
CHARLES SCRIBNER AND COMPANY.
1872.

RIVERSIDE, CAMBRIDGE:
STEREOTYPED AND PRINTED BY
H. O. HOUGHTON AND COMPANY.

PREFACE.

I HAVE prefixed to these Lectures a Sermon preached in Old Greyfriars' Church at the kind invitation of the Rev. Dr. Wallace, Minister of the Parish, on January 7, 1872. It indicates the spirit in which I would wish the subject in the Lectures to be approached, and on that account seemed a not unfitting introduction.

I have also wished to retain it as a record of the revival of a custom which had for a considerable period fallen into disuse, but which once was well recognized both in the Church of England and the Church of Scotland. It had long been my intention to avail myself of the liberty of preaching in the sister Church, which the law of both Churches allows, and had only waited till a fitting opportunity occurred. It is sufficient in illustration of this liberty, to refer to the interesting passage at the close of the twentieth edition of Dean Ramsay's "Reminiscences of Scottish Life," as regards the practice and feeling at the beginning of this century; to Bishop Ewing's admirable vindication of the principle in the "Sermon on Christmas-time," intended to have been preached before the University of Glasgow; and to Principal Tulloch's able essay on the "English and Scottish Churches" in the "Contemporary Review," in December, 1871. That such an event should have taken place without remonstrance or opposition in the Church of Scotland is a decisive proof of the liberality which, as I have remarked in the closing Lecture, is characteristic of its present condition.

The Lectures are printed as nearly as possible in their original state. Some inaccuracies of detail have been corrected, some ambiguities removed, and some passages which had been omitted for the sake of brevity have been retained.

I would venture here to repeat what was, in fact, implied throughout the Lectures, that they do not profess to give anything like a complete account of the history of the Scottish Church. Some of its most conspicuous personages, such as John Knox and Andrew Melville; some of its most conspicuous features, such as its system of education and of discipline; some of its most conspicuous events, the General Assembly of 1638, and the Disruption of 1843, — have been passed over, partly as sufficiently well known, partly for other reasons equally obvious.

I will add that I have also, on principle, abstained from entering into the details of the several controversies in which the Church of Scotland has been at different times involved. The particular points at issue between the Burghers and the Anti-burghers, between the Secession, the Relief, and the Free Church, between the Moderates and Populars, the Collegers, the Usagers, the Unionists and Anti-unionists, could only have been set forth by a minute investigation and exposition which would have diverted the attention from the general features of interest common to all of these divisions.

I have in my first Lecture indicated that the copiousness of the sources of Scottish ecclesiastical history, as well as the excellent modern works on the subject, render any lengthened narrative unnecessary. I do not pretend to more than a superficial knowledge of the vast literature which covers this field. But it may be convenient to give a brief summary of the chief works that can with advantage be consulted.

For the general history, I would specially name the compendious, but thoroughly liberal and well-digested "Church History of Scotland," from a Presbyterian point of view, in two volumes, by the Rev. John Cunningham, Minister of Crieff; and the exact and candid "Ecclesiastical History of Scotland," from an Episcopalian point of view, in four volumes, by Mr. George Grub; also the numerous notices of ecclesiastical affairs in Mr. Burton's elaborate "History of Scotland;" and the lucid exposition of all legal questions in Mr. Taylor Innes's admirable work on the "Law of Creeds in Scotland."

For the early Celtic period I would refer to Mr. Stuart's "Sculptured Stones of Scotland," and "The Book of Deer;" to Dr. Reeves's edition of Adamnan's "Life of Columba;" to Innes's "Early History of Scotland;" and to the modern reproduction of some of the chief characters in Montalembert's "Monks of the West." To these, it is to be hoped, will be shortly added Bishop Forbes's "Kalendar of the Lives of the early Scottish Saints."

For the mediæval period, I must repeat my deep obligations to the lamented Joseph Robertson, which began from the moment when I first became acquainted with him — of which none can have any adequate notion but those who had the privilege of conversing with him, but of which permanent traces are left in the singularly interesting "Essay on Scottish Abbeys and Cathedrals," in the eighty-fifth volume of the "Quarterly Review," and in the masterly Preface to the "Statuta Ecclesiæ Scotianæ." I would also name the "Sketches of Early Scottish History," by Mr. Cosmo Innes.

For the period of the Reformation, it is enough to mention the "History of the Reformation," by John Knox himself; the "Lives of John Knox and Andrew Melville," by Dr. M'Crie; the chapters relating to it in Froude's "History of England," and the Lectures on that and the succeeding period by Principal Lee.

For the period of the great struggle with the English State and hierarchy I would indicate Baillie's "Letters;" Wodrow's "History" and "Analecta;" the various Lives of Rutherford, Claverhouse, and Leighton, with the notices in Burnet's "Own Time," and Macaulay's "History of England."

For the period of the eighteenth century, I would specially refer to the Lives of Robertson and Blair, Sir H. Moncrieff Wellwood's "Life of Dr. John Erskine," Burton's "Life of David Hume," the Autobiographies of Dr. Carlyle, and Dr. Somerville, and of Thomas Boston, and the histories of the various secessions.

For the events near to our own time, it may perhaps suffice to mention Dr. Hanna's "Life of Chalmers," Mr. Herbert Story's Lives of "Story of Rosneath" and of "Robert Lee;" and Mrs. Oliphant's "Life of Edward Irving." To name the pamphlets and works relating to the Disruption of 1843 would be in itself a catalogue.

Of one other source of illustration I have freely availed myself, because in no other way could I so bring home the subject to the intelligence both of Englishmen and of Scotsmen, namely, the allusions to Scottish ecclesiastical history in the romances of "The Monastery," "The Abbot," "The Legend of Montrose," "Old Mortality," "The Heart of Mid-Lothian," "Redgauntlet," "The Antiquary," "Waverley," and "Guy Mannering." In no other like works of genius are the references to the religious feelings of the author's country so frequent; in none other is a knowledge of those feelings so necessary for a due understanding of the humor, the argument, and the characters that are produced.

In conclusion, I would here repeat what in substance I have elsewhere expressed, my regret if in any untoward remark I have wounded feelings which I would fain conciliate, not only from their intrinsic claim on my regard, but also from the kind indulgence I have received in Scotland even amongst the sections of the Church from which I most widely differ. If any such expressions still remain, I must plead in their behalf that in treading so fiery a soil it was almost impossible not to awaken some slumbering ashes; and that in so complex and interesting a subject it would have indicated a want of self-respect, and of respect for those whom I was addressing, if I had not touched, when required by the necessities of my argument, on the faults as well as on the virtues of the country in which I had the honor to be so generously welcomed; always with the endeavor (according to the rule laid down in the Address by which these Lectures are prefaced) to understand the truth which lay at the bottom of the error, and to make the best of whatever is admirable even in those from whom we are in other points the most divided.

CONTENTS.

"THE ELEVENTH COMMANDMENT."

LECTURE I.

THE CELTIC, THE MEDIÆVAL, AND THE EPISCOPAL CHURCHES.

LECTURE II.

THE CHURCH OF SCOTLAND, THE COVENANT, AND THE SECEDING CHURCHES.

LECTURE III.

THE MODERATION OF THE CHURCH OF SCOTLAND.

LECTURE IV.

THE PRESENT AND THE FUTURE OF THE CHURCH OF SCOTLAND.

"THE ELEVENTH COMMANDMENT."

SERMON PREACHED IN OLD GREYFRIARS' CHURCH, EDINBURGH, ON JANUARY 7, 1872.

THE ELEVENTH COMMANDMENT.

"*A new commandment I give unto you.*" — JOHN xiii. 34.

The Eleventh Commandment of the world.

WE all know the Ten Commandments. Is there such a thing as a new commandment — an Eleventh Commandment? We sometimes hear in conversation of such an Eleventh Commandment invented by the world, in cynical contempt of the old commands, or in pursuit of some selfish or wicked end. Of such an Eleventh Commandment, whether in jest or earnest, we need not here speak. It is enough to be reminded of it, and pass it by. But there is also what may be called the Eleventh Commandment of churches and sects.

The Eleventh Commandment of the Samaritan sect.

In the oldest and most venerable of all ecclesiastical divisions — the ancient Samaritan community, who have for centuries, without increase or diminution, gathered round Mount Gerizim as the only place where men ought to worship — there is to be read upon the aged parchment-scroll of the Pentateuch this commandment, added to the other Ten: "Thou shalt build an altar on Mount Gerizim, and there only shalt thou worship." Faithfully have they followed that command; excommunicating, and excommunicated by, all other religious societies, they cling to that eleventh command as equal, if not superior, to all the rest. This is the true likeness of what all churches and sects, unless purified by a higher spirit, are tempted to add. "Thou shalt do something for this particular community, which none else may share. Thou shalt do this over and above, and more than thy plain, simple duties to God and man. Thou shalt build thine altar on Mount Gerizim, for here alone our fathers have said that God is to be worshipped. Thou shalt maintain the exclusive sacredness of this or that place, this or that word, this or that doctrine, this or that party, this or that institution, this or that mode of doing good. Thou shalt worship God thus and thus only." This is the Eleventh Commandment according to sects and parties and partisans. For this we are often told to contend more than for all the other Ten together. For an Eleventh Commandment like to this, half the energies of Christendom have been spent, and spent in vain. For some command like this men have fought and struggled and shed their own blood and the blood of others, as though it were a command engraven on the tables of the everlasting law; and yet, again and again and again, it has been found in after ages that such a command was an addition as venerable, perhaps, and as full of interest, but as superfluous, as misleading, as disproportionate, as that Eleventh Samaritan commandment: "Thou shalt build an altar on Mount Gerizim, and there only shalt thou worship."

The Eleventh Commandment of the Christian religion.

But there is yet another Eleventh Commandment, not of the world, nor yet of mere churches or sects — the true Eleventh commandment of the Christian Religion. I have spoken of that Samaritan commandment as I have seen it far away in the sunny vale of Shechem, beneath the gray cliffs of Mount Gerizim. May I introduce this Christian commandment by a scene nearer home, within the bounds of your own kingdom and Church of Scotland; a story known doubtless to many amongst you, but which a stranger may be permitted to recall. There may be some here present who have visited the retired Vale of Anwoth, on the shores of Galloway. In the seventeenth century the minister of the parish of Anwoth was the famous Samuel Rutherford, the great religious oracle of the Covenanters and their adherents. It was, as all readers of his letters will remember, the spot which he most loved on earth. The very swallows and sparrows which found their nests in the church of Anwoth were, when far away, the objects of his affectionate envy. Its hills and valleys were the witnesses of his ardent devotion when living; they still retain his memory with unshaken fidelity. It is one of the traditions thus cherished on the spot, that on a Saturday evening, at one of those family gatherings whence, in the language of the great Scottish poet,

"Old Scotia's grandeur springs,'

when Rutherford was catechizing his children and servants, that a stranger knocked at the door of the manse, and (like the young English traveller in the celebrated romance which has given fresh life to those same hills in our own age) begged shelter for the night. The minister kindly received him, and asked him to take his place amongst the family and assist at their religious exercises. It so happened that the question in the catechism which came to the stranger's turn was that which asks, "How many commandments are there?" He answered "Eleven." "Eleven!" exclaimed Rutherford, "I am surprised that a man of your age and appearance should not know better. What do you mean?" And he answered, "A new commandment I give unto you, that ye love one another; as I have loved you, that ye also love one another. By this shall all men know that ye are my disciples, if ye have love one to another." Rutherford was much impressed by the answer, and they retired to rest. The next morning he rose early to meditate on the services of the day. The old manse of Anworth stood — its place is still pointed out — in the corner of a field, under the hill-side, and thence a long, winding, wooded path, still called Rutherford's Walk, leads to the church. Through this glen he passed, and, as he threaded his way through the thicket, he heard amongst the trees the voice of the stranger at his morning devotions. The elevation of the sentiments and of the expressions convinced him that it was no common man. He accosted him, and the traveller confessed to him that he was no other than the great divine and scholar, Archbishop Usher, the Primate of the Church of Ireland, one of the best and most learned men of his age, who well fulfilled that new commandment in the love which he won and which he bore to others; one of the few links of Christian charity between the fierce contending factions of that time, devoted to King Charles I. in his life-time, and honored in his grave by the Protector Cromwell. He it was, who, attracted by Rutherford's fame, had thus come in disguise to see him in the privacy of his own home.

The stern Covenanter welcomed the stranger prelate; side by side they pursued their way along Rutherford's Walk to the little church, of which the ruins still remain; and in that small Presbyterian sanctuary, from Rutherford's rustic pulpit, the archbishop preached to the people of Anwoth on the words which had so startled his host the evening before: "A new commandment I give unto you, that ye love one another; as I have loved you, that ye also should love one another."

Let me, on this occasion, humbly endeavor to follow the example of that illustrious prelate, and leaving the old eleventh commandment of the Samaritan sect, say a few words on the new eleventh commandment of the Christian Church.

I. Its original meaning.

I. Let me speak first of its original meaning. If we can easily imagine the surprise of the pious Scotsman when he first heard of an eleventh commandment, much more may we figure to ourselves the surprise of the Apostles when they, for the first time, heard this new announcement from the lips of their Divine Master. "What? Are not the Ten Commandments enough? Must we always be pressing forward to something new? What is this that He saith, 'A new commandment?' We cannot tell what He saith."

True it is that on those old Ten Commandments, much more on the two great commandments, hang all the law and the prophets. They contain the landmarks of our duty — the landmarks of our religion. But there is yet a craving in the human heart for something even beyond duty, even beyond reverence. There is a need which can only be satisfied by a new, by an eleventh commandment, which shall be at once old and new — which shall open a new field of thought and exertion for each generation of men; which shall give a fresh, undying impulse to its older sisters — the youngest child (so to speak) of the patriarchal family, the youngest and holiest and best gift of Him who has kept the good wine till the last. Many a false eleventh commandment, as I have said, has been put forth by the world to supply this want in its way; many a false eleventh commandment has been put forth by the churches in their way. But the true new commandment which our Saviour gave was, in its very form and fashion, peculiarly characteristic of his way — peculiarly characteristic of the Christian religion.

The novelty of the commandment lay in two points. First, it was new, because of the paramount, predominant place which it gave to the force of the human affections, the enthusiasm for the good of others, which was, — instead of ceremonial, or mere obedience, or correctness of belief, — henceforth to become the appointed channel of religious fervor. And secondly it was new, because it was founded on the appearance of a new character, a new manifestation of the character of Man, a new manifestation of the character of God. Even if the Four Gospels had been lost, we should see, from the urgency with which the Apostles press this new grace of Love or Charity upon us, that some diviner vision of excellence had crossed their minds. The very word which they used to express it was new, for the thing was new, the example was new, and the consequences therefore were new also. "Love one another," was the doctrine of Jesus Christ, "as I have loved you."

The solid blocks or tables on which the Ten Commandments were written were of the granite rock of Sinai, as if to teach us that all the great laws of duty to God, and duty to man, were like that oldest primeval foundation of the world — more solid, more enduring than all the other strata; cutting across all the secondary and artificial distinctions of mankind; heaving itself up, now here, now there; throwing up the fantastic crag, there the towering peak, here the long range which unites or divides the races of mankind. That is the universal, everlasting character of Duty. But as that granite rock itself has been fused and wrought together by a central fire, without which it could not have existed at all, so also the Christian law of Duty, in order to perform fully its work in the world, must have been warmed at the heart, and fed at the source by a central fire of its own — and that central fire is Love — the gracious, kindly, generous, admiring, tender movements of the human affections; and that central fire itself is kept alive by the consciousness that there has been in the world a Love beyond all human love, a devouring fire of Divine enthusiasm on behalf of our race, which is the Love of Christ, which is of the inmost essence of the Holy Spirit of God. It is not contrary to the Ten Commandments. It is not outside of them, it is within them; it is at their core; it is wrapped up in them, as the particles of the central heat of the globe were encased within the granite tables in the Ark of the Temple.

This was what the Apostle Paul meant by saying, "Love is the fulfilling of the Law." This is what St. Peter meant by saying, "Above all things, have fervent," enthusiastic "Love." This is what St. John meant when, in his extreme old age, he was carried into the market-place of Ephesus, and, according to the ancient tradition, repeated over and over again to his disciples the words which he had heard from his Master, "Little children, love one another." They were vexed by hearing this commandment, this Eleventh Commandment, repeated so often. They asked for something more precise, more definite, more dogmatic; but the aged Apostle, we are told, had but one answer: "This is the sum and substance of the Gospel; if you do this, I have nothing else to teach you." He did not mean that ceremonies, doctrines, ordinances were of no importance; but that they were altogether of secondary importance. He meant that they were on the outside of religion, whereas this commandment belonged to its innermost substance; that, if this commandment were carried out, all that was good in all the rest would follow; that if this commandment were neglected, all that was good in all the rest would fade away, and all that was evil, and one-sided, and exaggerated, would prevail and pervert even the good. He meant, and his Master meant, that as the ages rolled on, other truths may be folded up and laid aside; but that this would always need to be enforced and developed.

This, then, is the new commandment; we are to love one another, by making the best of one another; by seeing, as far as we can, their better side.

"He that will live in peace and rest
Must see and hear and say the best."

So says an ancient proverb, which well expresses the

meaning of this divine command. The new commandment was not, "Agree with one another in opinion or in form." It was not, as often has been said in the name of religion, "Hate, kill, extirpate one another." It was not, as in our weakness we often say, "Flatter, indulge, yield, to one another." It was not, as might in one sense well be said, "Teach one another, or govern one another." The command was, "Love one another." Love one another in spite of your differences, in spite of your faults, in spite of the excesses of one or the defects of another. Love one another, and make the best of one another, as He loved us, who, for the sake of saving what was good in the human soul, forgot, forgave, put out of sight what was bad — who saw and loved what was good even in the publican Zaccheus, even in the penitent Magdalen, even in the expiring malefactor, even in the heretical Samaritan, even in the Pharisee Nicodemus, even in the heathen soldier, even in the outcast Canaanite. Make the most of what there is good in institutions, in opinions, in communities, in individuals. It is very easy to do the reverse, to make the worst of what there is of evil, absurd, and erroneous. By so doing we shall have no difficulty in making estrangements more wide, and hatreds and strifes more abundant, and errors more extreme. It is very easy to fix our attention only on the weak points of those around us, to magnify them, to irritate them, to aggravate them; and, by so doing, we can make the burden of life unendurable, and can destroy our own and others' happiness and usefulness wherever we go. But this was not the love wherewith Christ loved us; this is not the new love wherewith we are to love one another. That love is universal, because in its spirit we overcome evil simply by doing good. We drive out error simply by telling the truth. We strive to look on both sides of the shield of truth. We strive to speak the truth in love, that is, without exaggeration or misrepresentation; concealing nothing, compromising nothing, but with the effort to understand each other, to discover the truth which lies at the bottom of error; with the determination cordially to love whatever is lovable even in those in whom we cordially detest whatever is detestable. And, in proportion as we endeavor to do this, there may be a hope that men will see that there are, after all, some true disciples of Christ left in the world, "because they have love one to another."

Application of the Eleventh Commandment to the divisions of churches.

II. Such is the original of the Eleventh Commandment, as it was first delivered by Christ and his Apostles. It is in one sense old, for it has been in the world for eighteen centuries. Yet in another sense it is always new, for it often has been superseded, even amongst Christians, by that old Samaritan commandment of which I spoke at the beginning. It is always new, for it admits and demands ever fresh applications to the circumstances of every Christian congregation, every Christian nation, and every Christian Church. May I, on this occasion, pass by the application to individuals and to nations, and fix your attention for a few moments on the new impulse, the new facilities which we possess for fulfilling the love which different churches ought to have one towards another, loving each other, even as Christ loved them all.

(1.) Better mutual appreciation.

(1.) First, this love does not imply the necessity of absorbing one church into another, or of destroying one church in order to make room for another. It consists — and herein the tendencies of our age give us an immense assistance in carrying out the new commandment — it consists in a better understanding, a better appreciation of the peculiar spirit of every church — in recognizing the peculiar semblance which exists under outward divergencies. For this discharge of our Christian duty, the increased knowledge of our past history, the increased means of personal communication, are homely, but not less sacred channels through which this grace may flow in and out on all the various sections of Christendom. It was a just remark of a veteran statesman and historian of France, in speaking of the electric effect produced on the fiercest of the leaders of the old Revolution by being suddenly, and for the first time, brought into close contact with the unfortunate Queen: "How many estrangements, misunderstandings, mortal enmities, would be cleared up and dispelled, if the adversaries could, for a few moments, meet eye to eye and face to face." Not less true is this of ecclesiastical than of political hostilities. The more we see of each other, the more we know of each other, the less possible is it to believe each other to be out of the pale of Christian salvation, or Christian sympathy; the more necessary does it become, in thinking and in speaking of the present ecclesiastical state and the future eternal state of the divided churches, to "bear all things, believe all things, hope all things, endure all things" of those whom, in the times of our mutual ignorance, we regarded as aliens from the commonwealth of Israel, and strangers from the covenants of promise.

(2.) Larger and deeper theology.

(2.) Secondly, this love, this increased intercourse and appreciation, does not imply the disparagement or the discouragement of Christian truth or Christian theology, in the proper sense of those words. On the contrary, it is the necessary consequence of the larger growth and deeper root which true Christian theology has taken, and may yet more fully take, in the circumstances of our time. Not without reason did the venerable patriarch of German Catholic theology, when, addressing a short time since the University of Munich, declare that of all the sciences that which would gain most from the impetus of modern events was Theology, which must henceforth "transform her mission from a mission of polemics into a mission of irenics; which, if it be worthy of the name, must become a science, not, as heretofore, for making war, but for making peace, and thus bring about that reconciliation of churches for which the whole civilized world is longing." It is but a natural result of the deeper study of the several parts of the Bible, according to the intention, meaning, and force of each — that the inward spirit and meaning of Christian truth should be seen athwart and beneath the outer forms in which the necessary development of later times has encompassed it. It is but the natural result of the increasing age of the world, that it should learn that temperance in theological argument, that better sense of proportion in theological statements, which we sometimes see in the increased moderation of the experience of individuals, in the mildness of the mellowed old age of Athanasius and Augustine, of Luther, of Baxter, and of Wesley. It is but the natural result wherever lofty intellectual powers, or powerful spiritual discernment, have turned on theological subjects. The religious thoughts of Bacon, Butler, and Berkeley, of Shakespeare, Milton, and Walter Scott; or, again, of Pascal and Thomas à Kempis; or, again, coming down to a lower level, of Bishop Wilson's Maxims, or Whichcote's Aphorisms; or yet, again, the sermons of Frederick Robertson in the Church of England, and the "pastoral counsels" of John Robertson in the Church of Scotland, alike lead us to that peaceful path of true wisdom "which the lion's whelp hath not trodden nor the vulture's eye seen" — which the fierce fanatic hath not known, nor the jealous polemic guarded.

(3.) Union for great objects.

(3.) Thirdly, the true union between Christian Churches promoted by the deepening sense — deepening in all that have eyes to see or ears to hear the signs of the time — the deepening sense of the mighty works that have to be achieved, and that may be achieved, for the moral and social regeneration of mankind. There are unions between churches that are often proposed as mere strategic operations against some church or party which we dread or dislike.[1] Such strategy may be needed; for, in this mixed world, we must ever be more or less militant. But with operations of this kind the new commandment of Christian love has no special concern. It is when we see some union formed for high philanthropic objects, or inspired by a common feeling of sympathy for what is in itself just, noble,

[1] See Lecture IV.

and true, that we recognize a sample of what ought to be the animating principle of the true fraternal unity of churches. "Nothing," says a philosophic observer of our own time, "produces such steadfast friendships as working together for some public good." Nothing so fuses together all differences as some event which evokes the better side of human nature in large masses of men. Few could fail to be struck by the sudden transformation of the whole British nation into a people with one heart and one soul, in the recent combination of personal compassion and national sentiment called out by the anxiety for the safety of the heir to the English throne. Such an example is a likeness of what might be effected by a loyal, universal enthusiasm on behalf of the great principles of truth, justice, and beneficence, which are the true objects of the devotion of Christendom. The age of the Crusades, for which Robert the Bruce sought to give his heart's blood, is past and gone. But there are causes of Christian charity far holier than that for which the Crusaders fought, which might call forth more than the Crusaders' chivalry. The Solemn League and Covenant is dead and buried; but the New Commandment, which bids us unite instead of dividing, and build up instead of destroying, is a league far more sacred, a covenant far more binding than any which your forefathers ever signed with their blood, or followed to death or victory. The famous Confession of Faith which issued from Westminster in the seventeenth century, as the expression of the whole Church and nation of Great Britain — noble and inspiring though it was, in some respects beyond all the confessions of Protestant Europe — is yet not to be compared with the uniting and sanctifying force of the Christian English literature which in the nineteenth century has become the real bond and school of the nation, beyond the power of educational or ecclesiastical agitation to exclude or to pervert.

Associations of Greyfriars' Church.

Such are some of the manifold ways in which the Eleventh Commandment may in this age be fulfilled as never before. And surely it may be said, that if there be any spot where, should the preacher be silent on this great theme, the very stones would immediately cry out, it is this venerable sanctuary. Of Greyfriars' Church and churchyard, as of my own Abbey of Westminster, it may truly be said, that it is the consecrated temple of reconciled ecclesiastical enmities. Here, as there, the silence of Death breathes the lesson which the tumult of life hardly suffered to be heard. In the same ground with the martyrs of the Covenant lies the great advocate by whose counsel their blood was shed.[1] Within the same hallowed bounds sleep the wise leaders of the Church of Scotland in the next generation, whom the persecutors and the persecuted of an earlier age would alike have condemned. And not only is this lesson of larger, gentler, more discriminating justice forced upon us by the thought of that judgment-seat before which these all are passed; but the memory also of the deeds which have been wrought within these precincts impresses the same truth upon us. Here it was that Episcopalian ministers shed tears of grateful sorrow over the grave

[1] See Lecture III.

of Carstairs; here Erskine, with generous candor, preached the funeral eulogy over his ecclesiastical rival, William Robertson. On this spot, where a vast congregation of every age and rank pledged themselves against every form and shade of Prelacy, the Scottish Church has, in these latter days, had the courage to revive the ancient forms of liturgical worship, and welcome the ministrations of Episcopalian clergy.

These contrasts are of themselves sufficient to remind us how transitory are the feuds which have in earlier days rent asunder the churches of these islands — how eternal are the bonds which unite them, when viewed in the light of history, and as before the judgment of a higher world. And if the ghosts of the ancient disputes have been here laid to sleep, never, we trust, to return — if the coming of a brighter age, and the opening of a wider horizon, has dawned from time to time on the teachers, famous in their generation, who have ministered within these walls — then, I trust, it will not have been unsuitable that in this place, and on this occasion, a Scottish congregation should have heard from an English churchman, the best New Year's blessing under the form of this sacred text: "A new commandment I give unto you, that ye should love one another."

LECTURE I.

THE CELTIC, THE MEDIÆVAL, AND THE EPISCOPAL CHURCH.

DELIVERED BEFORE THE PHILOSOPHICAL INSTITUTE,

JANUARY 8, 1872.

LECTURE I.

THE CELTIC, THE MEDIÆVAL, AND THE EPISCOPAL CHURCH.

It requires some courage in an Englishman to address a Scottish audience on a subject so peculiarly their own as the Church of Scotland. The motto of your own thistle, "Nemo me impune lacessit," might almost be rendered in regard to the Scottish Church, — "No one has ever meddled with it without repenting of it." And this apprehension might be yet further increased, when it is remembered that I appear before you as the representative of a prelatical hierarchy, as an Erastian of the Erastians. But I gather confidence from the kind indulgence which I have received from all sections of the Scottish Church, and I venture to premise that in the plan which I propose to take I find some grounds of encouragement.

Plan of the lectures.

It is not my intention to attempt any narrative of Scottish ecclesiastical history. Even were it possible for me to do so, it is unnecessary. No part of the British islands has had the history of its Church so fully told as Scotland.[1] Assuming, therefore, in my audience a knowledge of the general facts, all that I now propose is to call attention to such leading features as serve as landmarks to the whole.

[1] See Preface to the Lectures.

In speaking of the Church of Scotland, I shall have occasion in my following lectures to show more at length that the only strict and legitimate sense in which the word can be applied is in reference to the National Church of Scotland, as established by law. But it so happens that in Scotland this expression takes a wider range than the corresponding phrases either in England or Ireland. There are at present what may be called three Churches in Scotland,—the Established Church, the Dissenting Presbyterian Churches, and the Dissenting Episcopalian Churches; and the course of my lectures will follow these divisions. But, nevertheless, such a distinct demarcation as this would be misleading. However much the Scottish nation has been broken up by religious divisions, these divisions have not only not broken up the unity of the nation, but they have not altogether broken up the unity of the Church. There is a true sense in which the Established Church, the different Seceding Churches, and the Episcopalian Churches, are all parts of one and the same Church of Scotland — a sense truer than that in which this might possibly be said of the Three[1] Irish Churches, or of the Church of England in relation to the numerous churches and sects which surround it. The three forms of Scottish belief and church government have at different times so overlapped and run across each other, that there have been periods when, without any straining of language, each one of them might have been called the Church or the religion of Scotland. And yet more, the different elements specially

[1] See Lecture on "The Three Irish Churches," in *Essays on Church and State*, p. 379.

characteristic of each, are in varying proportions characteristic also of the whole. There are Scottish traits which are never lost in any of them; there are peculiarities which might seem to belong only to one or other of these forms, but which yet reappear in each of the three. The tartan is the same throughout; it is only the red, the blue, or the green that are differently adjusted.

It need hardly be said, that an ecclesiastical history where such affinities can be traced is exceedingly instructive, as showing how the true grounds of union or disunion underlie the superficial grounds of either. And when from the relations of the different Scottish communions towards each other we pass to their common relations to other churches, a new interest arises from the strongly marked, almost grotesque exaggeration in which these different forms represent the ecclesiastical virtues and vices which in a fainter or milder aspect appear in other communions. An English High-churchman may be encouraged or discouraged, as the case may be, at finding himself reproduced in vivid colors by a Scottish Free-churchman or Covenanter. An English Nonconformist may be warned or stimulated by seeing his likeness in an Anti-burgher, or a Cameronian. An English Latitudinarian may be comforted or troubled, as the case may be, by finding his close affinity with a Scottish Moderate. The well-known wish of the great Scottish poet is fulfilled by the lessons of Scottish church history: —

> "O that some fay the gift would gie us,
> To see ourselves as others see us."

Perhaps the Scotsman may derive some of the blessings of this gift, when he hears himself described by an Englishman. Certainly the Englishman may derive some of those blessings by seeing himself, as the case may be, caricatured or transfigured by a Scotsman.

Plan of the present lectures.

I propose, then, in the following lectures, to endeavor to bring out some of these points in the different departments of Scottish history. The present lecture will be devoted to the somewhat complicated task of passing in review the early condition of Scottish religion. In so doing, it will be my object to obtain some glimpses into the ancient elements out of which the present ecclesiastical condition has arisen; to show the identity of customs and sentiments between the earliest and the latest stages; to mark the influence from first to last exercised by the southern kingdom through these channels, and to exhibit through the successive stages the development of Episcopacy in Scotland, and the extremely entangled state of its relations to Presbyterianism.

It is obvious that this can only be done in a discursive and disjointed manner, but the subject within the prescribed limits admits of no other treatment.

The Celtic Church.

The first period, then, is that of the earliest beginnings of Scottish Christianity, from the fourth to the eleventh century. Let me first speak of the outward frame-work of the ecclesiastical constitution. The relation of early Presbyterianism to early Episcopacy in Scotland is the more worth discussing because it forms part of a larger system which prevailed throughout Celtic Christendom. That there were persons bearing the name of bishop in the earliest Christian history of Scotland is undoubted.[1] But it is equally undoubted that they had no dioceses, no jurisdiction, no territorial episcopal succession. Their orders were repudiated by the prelates of England and France.[2] The primate of the Church of Scotland for the first three hundred years of its history was not a bishop but a presbyter — first the abbot of Iona,[3] then of Dunkeld. The succession was a succession, not of Episcopal hands, but of a dead presbyter's relics.[4] Early bishops of St. Andrew's, Glasgow, and the like, figure in legends, but they had no existence in fact.[5] The abbot, not the bishop, was regarded as the ordinary ecclesiastical ruler, and the superiors of the various monasteries, by which the country was evangelized, looked to the chief abbot as the head of their whole church. It was, in fact, the same system as that which prevailed in the ancient Irish Church,[6] of which some traces are still, even in the Latin Churches, to be seen in the all but episcopal power of the great Benedictine abbots of Monte Casino and La Cava.

The abbatial system.

Thus much is acknowledged by all. It may be more doubtful, but it is still the most obvious inference from Bede's[7] narrative, that the abbots and presbyters of Iona actually ordained or consecrated the bishops whom they sent forth to England; and it is therefore exceedingly probable that the episcopal succession of the northern provinces of England

1 Grub, i. 139.

2 Ibid. 127, 128.

3 Ibid. 135.

4 Ibid. 131.

5 This is well put in Burton's *History of Scotland*, i. 281.

6 Ibid. 14. Lecture on the "Three Irish Churches." *Essays on Church and State*, 382, 383.

7 Bede, iv. 3, 5. This inference is contended by Mr. Grub (i. 151–157) in an able but not conclusive argument.

has been deeply colored by Presbyterian blood. It was the belief of the chief Scottish chronicler of the Middle Ages that these same exalted presbyters consecrated[1] bishops, and crowned and consecrated kings. The first Christian rite of coronation is, in fact, derived from Columba's coronation of the Celtic Chief of the Hebrides.[2] That which in England was believed to be so inalienable a prerogative of the see of Canterbury that Becket shed his blood rather than concede it even to his brother primate of York,[3] was in Scotland yielded without a struggle by the whole of the Scottish Episcopate to a wild abbot fresh from Ireland.

It is not to be inferred from this account, that the early ecclesiastical system of Scotland was like the modern. It was, no doubt, as unlike modern Presbyterianism as it was unlike modern Episcopacy. The abbots were not bishops, but they were prelates. They were presbyters, but they had no presbyteries. Still it is possible that the subtle influence which ancient institutions exercise over far distant ages may in this case have been not without its effect, and that when the earthquake came in which Episcopacy perished, the Scottish soil had been to a certain degree prepared for its overthrow, by the fact that the earliest evangelizers had not been bishops.

The vitality of the early saints.

There is another peculiar characteristic of this early period, which is specially to be seen in Scotland. Whatever remains there were of the early Celtic saints of England have

[1] Fordun's *Scoti-Chronicon*, vi. 49; Grub. i. 159.

[2] Adamnan, iii. 5. Martene, ii. 213.

[3] *Memorials of Canterbury*, 68, 69, 78, 90, 125.

long since perished. The one solitary name which figures in the ancient Christian history of England, is the martyr of the Roman city of Verulam, St. Alban. After him, no other ecclesiastical association exists, legendary or historical, if we except the obscure saints of Cornwall and Wales, till we reach Augustine. The memories of St. Botolph and St. Dunstan, of St. Edmund and St. Edward, although they retained a strong influence during long tracts of the Middle Ages, can hardly be said to have maintained their vitality to our own time. But in Scotland, even in spite of the vast counter wave of the Reformation, the local attractions of these primitive missionaries still hold their ground, and their successive apparitions may well recall for a moment the various stages of the original Celtic faith. The first figure that distinctly emerges from the mists of fable in the pages [1] of Bede is the Cumbrian or Galwegian saint of the White House, the first stone church of the Roman camp of Leucophibia or Whithorn.[2] We can still see the ruined chapel on the lonely island promontory, the yet more ancient priory where his remains repose — once the spot to which kings and princes came [3] in pilgrimage across the trackless wilds of Galloway long after such toilsome devotions had ceased in England. We can explore the cave called by his name, which opens

1 Bede, iii. 4. Grub, i. 12.

2 Is not "Whithorn" and possibly "Candida Casa" simply the Anglicized and Latinized form of Leucophibia?

3 Mr. Stuart of the Register House, Edinburgh, will, I trust, permit these slight recollections of the instructive intercourse with him during a delightful visit to the "holy places" of Galloway, in 1871, when he discovered the cross mentioned in the lecture.

from beneath the samphire-covered cliff, undermined by the waves of Glenluce Bay; and on which a rudely carved cross still marks the original sanctity of the spot; where, following the practice of his master, St. Martin of Tours, he may well have retired for his devotions. These, and the churches and chapels which bear his name throughout Scotland are standing monuments of the once wide-spread power of the name of St. Ninian; and to him alone, of all British saints, a coeval monument still points in unmistakable characters. Nowhere in Great Britain is there a Christian record so ancient as the gray weather-beaten column which now serves as the gate-post of the deserted churchyard of Kirk Madreen[1] on the bleak hill in the centre of the Rinns of Galloway, and bearing on its battered surface, in letters of the fourth century,[2] the statement that it had marked the graves of three saints of Gallic name, Florentius, Vincentius, and Mavorius. Few, very few, have been the travellers that have reached that secluded monument; long may it stand as the first authentic trace of Christian civilization in these islands.

St. Ninian.

Or, to pass from Galloway to Fifeshire, where in England shall we find a hermitage so venerable as the caves which St. Serf scooped out for himself on the craggy "desert"[3] of the shores of the Firth of Forth, or on the romantic spot marked

St. Serf.

1 Doubtless Mathurinus, the disciple (according to the Roman Hagiology) of St. Martin of Tours, with whom, according to Bede, St. Ninian himself had passed some time on his return from Rome.

2 It is given at length in Mr. Stuart's *Sculptured Stones of Scotland.* Plate lxxi. p. 36.

3 "Desertum," the modern "Dysart."

by the little chapel beneath the wooded hill of Culross, where he discovered the infant Kentigern, his darling Mungo? Or, if we carry on the story of that wondrous child, what city of Great Britain bears, as its heraldic emblems, such a train of legendary associations as in the three miracles of St. Kentigern still retained on the shield of the great commercial city of Glasgow?[1] Or what scene of ancient British missionary labors can we so vividly represent to ourselves as the circle of venerable trees on the banks of the Molendinar,[2] under whose shade sprang up the wooden church which the same Kentigern erected as the centre of that Cumbrian Christianity, which reached from St. Asaph to Stirling.

St. Mungo.

And as we are led on, not by an episcopal but a true apostolical succession, from one of these saints to another, the legend of St. Kentigern carries us on to the first distinct and definite personage of the Scottish Church. To his retreat above the brawling millstream in what was even then a consecrated graveyard — the first germ of that vast cemetery, whence the statue of John Knox looks down over the teeming city of Glasgow[3] — came, according to tradition, to exchange their pastoral staves, the Abbot of Iona, the founder of the hierarchy which lasted for four hundred years, St. Columba. "The way of the holy hath been made light," said the one. "The holy shall go," cried the other, "from strength to strength — they all shall appear in Zion."[4]

1 Burton, i. 24.

2 See the admirable article on "Scottish Abbeys and Cathedrals," by the lamented Joseph Robertson, in the *Quarterly Review*, lxxxv. 130.

3 Ibid.

4 Montalembert's *Monks of the West. Moines de l' Occident*, iii. 325.

Let me say a few words concerning Iona, and concerning Columba.

The natural features and the Celtic names still preserved in Iona[1] give us the complete frame-work of the earliest authentic history of Scottish Christianity. We can trace Columba's arrival and sojourn here almost step by step. The northern coast of Ireland and the western coast of Caledonia were to the dwellers on either side almost as one country—both were regarded as the land of the Scots. From the promontories of Antrim the Scottish shores are completely visible. When Columba left his native glens in Donegal, and his dear familiar oak groves of Derry, a banished, excommunicated man, these shores were to him the natural outlet of his zeal. He was to leave his own island; but whilst he sought the nearest sphere of his future labors, it must also be one which placed him beyond the temptation of returning home. In the Hebridean group, the first which he reached was that formed by Jura with its three craggy "Paps," and the two islands now called, we can hardly doubt, from himself and his companion, Colonsay[2] and Oransay. But from Colonsay Ireland was still visible. He could not trust himself within view of it. He, with his twelve companions, in their frail coracle, embarked

Columba.

Iona.

1 I have given here the results of a personal investigation of the localities of Iona in the summer of 1869. Since that time the results of a yet more extended investigation of the island and its history has been published in a charming little volume by its present noble owner, the Duke of Argyll; to which I gladly refer for more complete details on the subject.

2 The parallel with *Oransay* seems decisive as to the explanation, and though Colonsay is called "Coloso" by Adamnan, this can only be from the attempt to Latinize it.

once more. They pushed on across the open sea. In front there rose a pyramidal hill, which seemed to beckon them on. It was Dun-I, "the hill of I, or Hy." At the south end of the island there is a bay deep withdrawn behind a group of rocky islets that stand out above the waves. Between these rocks Columba drove his coracle, and found himself on a beach of the pure white sand, which is the glory of the shores of Iona, sprinkled with the green serpentine pebbles which pilgrims and travellers have long carried off as trophies. This is still called the Port of the Coracle,[1] and beneath the long low mound, slightly fenced around with cairns and stones, sixty feet long, is said to lie buried the original bark. Overhanging this bay is a rocky hill,[2] which Columba climbed, and looked once more westward. Ireland was now invisible; he felt himself secure. From this point, which was henceforth to be called "the Hill with the Back turned on Ireland," he descended into the island which he was to make his own. He advanced across the low hills which part the Bay of the Coracle from the long plain which looks towards the Isle of Mull. Whatever may have led him in the first instance to Iona, it was the peculiarity of this plain which fixed his continuance there. He was in an island — removed from the immediate danger of attack from the savage Highland tribes —

[1] *Port-a-hurrach*, the Gaelic modification of "currach" in composition. When Johnson and Boswell came to the spot, they were perplexed by finding, as they thought, the English word *wherry* in *Port-a-wherry*. Boswell's *Johnson*, iii. 34.

[2] For these different allusions to the local features — *locus eminentior* — *in saltibus* — the ivy — the wooden structure of the huts, see Adamnan's *Life of Columba*.

but still sufficiently within reach of the main-land (for such the Isle of Mull may, comparatively speaking, be called) to communicate with its inhabitants, and to receive provisions and communications from them. The strait is so narrow that the human voice could be heard across; and one of the most frequent incidents in his life is that signals came of some expected or unexpected guest from the opposite shore. "Some one is coming over who will upset my ink-bottle;" and so it proved. Every trace of the actual habitations of Columba has perished; but so unchanged are the natural features of the place that we can fix, if not the very spot on which he pitched his little hut, yet the close neighborhood of it. It was, in all probability, the low knoll immediately above the humble inn of the modern village. There is a glen on the west of the island, over whose rocky walls hangs, in vast tresses, the ivy which was used to weave together the walls of the huts, built of the branches of thorn and briar which grow not far off. In this glen, and in others of like kind, Columba would retire at times from his little community to still deeper solitude. One of them is still called the Glen of the Temple, and leads to the corn plain on the other side of the island, still, as in Columba's time, bearing the name of Machar or "Sandy Plain;" out of the midst of this rise two green hills. It is curious that to these and not to the towering peak of Dun-I, is attached the legend which invests the island with its most peculiar sanctity. Columba, in one of the retreats of which we have spoken, withdrew into this plain, forbidding any of his disciples to follow him. One of them, more curious than the rest, climbed a rocky point which runs out into the plain, and from thence reported that he saw Columba on the larger of the two hills holding converse with the angels. After the lapse of a thousand years that eminence is still called the "Knoll of the Angels,"[1] the same name which was given to it from this association within a hundred years of its supposed occurrence. Nearer to the habitation of the saint cluster the local recollections of his last days. Winding along the slope of the shore, on which the little settlement was established, came the old white pony, which received his parting affectionate caresses on the eve of his death.[2] The scene of this event is in all probability marked by the one cross which remains standing in Iona, commonly called the cross of Maclean. Immediately above the settlement rises a singularly marked and prominent knoll, which commands the whole Strait of Mull. This hill, still called the Tor Ab, — the Hill of the Abbot, — the first to whom that venerable name was given, is, we cannot doubt, the little hill, "the Monticellus," which Columba, now enfeebled with age, climbed on the day before his death, and foretold its future fame.

His mission to Scotland.

What Columba was in Ireland I have elsewhere described.[3] What he was in Scotland is unfortunately lost in a tissue of unmeaning miracles. But there is no reason to doubt the highly characteristic tradition that the evangelization of Scotland was due in the first instance to a deadly

1 Cnoc Angel. It is also called the Great Hill of the Fairies, as the smaller hill is called the Little Hill of the Fairies. The story is told in Adamnan, iii. 16 (Reeves, 257).

2 Adamnan, iii. 23.

3 "The Three Irish Churches," *Lectures on Church and State*, pp. 384, 386.

quarrel between two Irish clans about the appropriation of a Psalter, and that the first apostle of Scotland was under the ban of the visible Church. The form which this part of the tradition assumes is full of interest.

A council of the Irish clergy had met and driven him forth as an excommunicated outcast. In the council — so runs the story — was one of the two mysterious Irish saints who bore the name of Brendan.[1] Saint Brendan, when the excommunicated man appeared in the council, rose up and embraced him. The whole council burst into exclamations of horror. "You would do as I have done," said Brendan; "and you would never have excommunicated him, if you saw what I see."[2]

Such excommunicated men have been seen in Scotland and in England often since. They may be seen at this moment in Rome, in Paris, and in Munich. There was a freedom and justice in this old Celtic conception of true greatness, which even at this day we have hardly obtained. Columba is not the only excommunicated man who, to the eyes of the truly discerning, has had beside him angels, and before him a pillar of fire. Brendan was right in thinking, "a pillar of fire before him and the angels of heaven beside him. I dare not disdain a man predestined

1 Not, I fear, the one who, as beautifully told in Matthew Arnold's *Poems*, in his Arctic voyages had seen and brought back the pathetic vision of Judas Iscariot, refreshing himself on the iceberg in the one day in every year, in which, for the one deed of mercy performed in his mortal life, he was allowed to retreat thither from the fires of hell.

2 This other was the elder St. Brendan, whose funeral, attended by angels, was seen in a vision by Columba when in Iona. Montalembert's *Moines de l' Occident*, iii. 135.

by God to be the guide of an entire people to eternal life."

It is a story which teems with instruction. His career remains a glorious proof how the ban of the visible Church against the moving spirits of mankind may turn out to be vanity of vanities. Whatever the shortcomings of Columba, St. Brendan was right in saying, that we cannot afford to "disdain a man predestined to be the evangelizer and apostle of such a nation as Scotland."

The other recollections of Iona are of a later age. The Martyrs' Bay — the white beach opposite to Mull, which derives its name from the massacre of the natives by Danish pirates, — is the spot on which the funeral processions from the surrounding islands have disembarked their mournful freights, and placed them on a rude mound at the curve of the shore. Thence they were borne, kings of Scotland, kings of Norway, lords of the Isles, to the cemetery consecrated by the neighborhood of Columba's bones, but deriving its name from his companion of dubious fame, the indiscreet Oran. It is the oldest regal cemetery of Great Britain — before Dunfermline, before Holyrood, before Westminster, before Windsor. It is, further, the most continuously ancient cemetery of the world. In none other have the remains of the dead been laid through an unbroken track of one thousand three hundred years, beginning with Columba and his companions, ending with the shipwrecked mariners of a few years ago.

The sanctity of Iona.

And as it is the most venerable cemetery of the Celtic race, so also is it marked by that singular characteristic of Celtic countries — the union of tenacious reverence with reckless neglect, which only within our own time the care of the present owner, worthy of the precious possession intrusted to his charge, has endeavored to rectify and prevent. With Oran's cemetery ends the true historic connection of Iona with Columba. The cathedral of Iona, with its Norman arches, carries us both by its style and its name to a region far removed from the first Celtic missionary. The architecture tells of its origin from the half Norman Margaret, under whose auspices the royal funerals were transferred from Iona to Dunfermline, indicating the transfer of sanctity from these western islands to the seat of Lowland government. The name of "cathedral" tells how far the Church of Scotland had, in the fourteenth century, drifted away from the days when the abbot of Iona was supreme over the Hebrides, and when no Episcopal chair had constituted any Scottish church into a cathedral. But of that long mediæval history of Iona nothing, or next to nothing, has come down to us. The last historic picture which the sacred island presents us is but within fifty years of Columba's death, when the French Bishop Arculf, driven by stress of weather on his return from the Holy Land, found a refuge in the humble tenement of the Abbot Adamnan, and where Adamnan took down from his mouth the only description of Palestine that exists between the fall of the Roman Empire and the Saracenic occupation. We see, as we read the disjointed record, the traveller telling, the abbot questioning, till the whole story was at last recorded in its present rude form.

Arculf and Adamnan.

It was not till the close of the eighteenth century that the fame of Columba once again attracted to these distant shores a pilgrim from the world of letters, as illustrious as ever was drawn from regal or episcopal thrones — and that the Holy Island received a new canonization in the immortal sentence which now springs to the memory of every educated Englishman when Iona is named.

Dr. Johnson.

"We were now treading that illustrious island which was once the luminary of the Caledonian regions. That man is little to be envied whose patriotism will not gain force on the plains of Marathon, or whose piety will not grow warmer among the ruins of Iona."

Before we finally quit this early period of the Scottish Church, I will venture to note two general features which link together the old and the new Scotland in a close connection often little suspected. One is the fertility and rapidity of development equally displayed in the miraculous legends of the ancient and modern saints of Scotland. The miracles of the early Scottish saints are not in themselves more fantastic or marvellous than those which adorn the hagiology of England, or the southern countries of Europe. But what gives them a singular interest is, that they are of the same kind as those which sprung up on the same soil twelve centuries later, in a theological atmosphere of the most opposite character. Even as regards the natural enthusiasm which gathered round their lives or their graves, there is no country in which the traveller passes, by such an immediate transition, from the saints of the

Miraculous stories of earlier and later Scottish saints.

fourth century to those of the seventeenth, as when in Galloway he comes fresh from the grave of St. Ninian at one end of the Wigtonshire promontory, to the graves of Margaret Maclachlan and Margaret Wilson, who sleep in the churchyard above the Bladenoch at the other end. And when we read, that in heavy showers of rain St. Ninian rode on without a drop falling on his book of devotions [1] except when a light thought passed through his mind, and that Robert Bruce the Covenanter made a long ride to Stirling under the same circumstances, perfectly dry, whilst his less godly companion was drenched to the skin, we feel at once that, though divided by the chasm of many generations, and by the widest revolutions of opinion, we are not only in the same physical atmosphere of endless mist and storm, but in the same spiritual [2] atmosphere of wild credulity and inexhaustible imagination. Nowhere can the vexed questions of the miracles of religious history be better discussed than in Scotland, because nowhere do they appear so impartially repeated under the most diverse phases of theological thought; because nowhere is it more evident that, whatever may be said either by orthodox or heterodox critics, historical facts can be disentangled from legendary accretions, and the repetition of the same incidents in these two most divergent epochs proves decisively that neither, on the one hand, do true facts necessitate the belief

[1] I owe this parallel to Mr. Stuart.

[2] It is believed in Morayshire that, at a funeral of a saint belonging to the so-called "Men," the Spey was miraculously dried up to enable the procession to cross just below the Boat of Garton Station, where a stone (since destroyed) was erected to commemorate the event. Nothing of the kind has occurred in England since the legend of St. Alban.

in the accompanying dubious miracles, nor, on the other, need the questioning of dubious miracles discredit the truth of the facts or the nobleness of the characters connected with them.

Reverence for sacramental ordinances in earlier and later times.

Another aspect of the same identity of sentiment between the earliest and the latest development of the Scottish Church is in regard to the doctrine of the Sacraments. Perhaps if there were any subject on which it might have been thought that the rent of the Reformation would have divided, by an impassable gulf, the past and the present history of Scotland, it would be the veneration for the Eucharist. Yet this is the very point in which a likeness starts to view such as would be vainly sought in any other country in Europe, over which a like change had passed. Let me give two examples. It was remarked in the eleventh century that one deeply-rooted feeling of the ancient Scottish Church, as represented by the Culdees, was the awful reverence for the sacrament, growing to such a pitch that from mere terror of the ordinance, it had ceased to be celebrated, even at the great festival of Easter.[1] Such a sentiment, so overleaping itself, has perhaps never been equaled again, except in the Scotland of the nineteenth century. Those who know the influence of the "Men" in the Highlands tell us that the same extravagant awe, causing an absolute repulsion from the sacred rite, is still to be found there.[2] Old gray-headed patriarchs are to be seen tottering with fear out of the church when the sacramental day comes round; many refusing to

1 Grub, i. 195, 196. For a beautiful picture of the true reverence of a Presbyterian Sacrament in Scotland, see Principal Shairp's poem of Kilmahoe.

2 Cunningham, i. 99.

be baptized, many more abstaining from the Eucharist altogether; and, at the time when the Veto Act was discussed, it was found incompatible with any regard to the rights of the parishioners to leave the election in the hands of the communicants, because in the extreme north (where the "Men" prevailed), out of a congregation of several thousands, the communicants, from motives of excessive reverence, did not exceed a hundred.[1]

The other is a more pleasing incident. It is recorded that a poor half-witted boy in Forfarshire[2] clamored incessantly to be allowed, as he expressed it, to partake of his Father's bread in the sacramental elements. At last the minister conceded the point. He partook; and the same night, on returning from the Sacrament, he kept repeating, in a rapture of reverence, "I have seen the Pretty Man." The next morning he was found dead in his bed.

Let those who think that what are called high views of the Eucharist are peculiar to Episcopalian or Catholic Churches consider how in this affecting story is contained the spiritual element of the same sentiment which, in its grosser shape, has given birth to the miracle of Bolsena and the excesses of Transubstantiation. Let those who think scorn of the humble Presbyterian ordinances reflect how in them the adoring veneration of the worshipper may be pitched in as lofty a key as beneath the dome of

[1] Turner's *History of the Secession*, pp. 182, 184.

[2] This strange incident has been turned into a little story, entitled *Yeddie's First and Last Sacrament*, and it is also told in Dean Ramsay's *Reminiscences*, 20th edit. p. 239. I had already heard the story from Mr. Erskine of Linlathen, and I have been told that it occurred at Tannadine, between Forfar and Kerriemuir.

St. Peter's, or amidst the splendor of copes and chasubles. Is it too much to suppose that a subterranean current of Christian feeling has linked together the child and the man of Scottish history in this respect, more evidently than in the regions where otherwise the break has been less violent?[1]

The Mediæval hierarchy.

II. The second phase of Scottish religion is that which dates from the establishment of the Anglo-Norman hierarchy by Queen Margaret, and continues down to the Reformation. There is one leading peculiarity of this period which, whilst it appears still more prominently in the third stage, on which we shall presently enter, belongs also in some degree to the first, which we are leaving.

Foreign influences.

Scotland is, in some respects, essentially self-contained, and on this depends a large part of its ecclesiastical history, as we shall see in my next lecture. Yet there is also a sense in which it is peculiarly dependent on other countries. Its geography almost lends itself to the connection. Look at the three long fingers of Galloway, reaching out into the sea till they almost clasp the coast of Cumberland and the Isle of Man, and even the shores of Ireland. The kingdom of Strath-Clyde embraced in its folds the Cumbrian Churches and tribes on both sides of the Solway. That wild estu-

[1] Even in detail some of the Eucharistic controversies which agitate Episcopal Churches have broken out on the like questions in Scotland. There was in the last century a long ritual dispute between a presbyter and his presbytery exactly analogous to that which was recently raised by the English ritualists and their opponents, respecting the elevation of the consecrated elements. It took the form of a schism between Lifters and Antilifters, which at last emerged in the Old and New Lights.

ary was not a dividing boundary, but a highway of communication for Ninian and for Kentigern (as well as for Bruce and for Guy Mannering) to traverse in their passage to and fro on their familiar journeys or look at the Border. Cuthbert was an English even more than he was a Scottish saint. His return from the highlands of Iona to his native lowlands of Melrose was a more decisive emigration than his wandering over the Cheviots of Lindisfarne. His own Eildon Hills brooded over him on the whole of his southern journey. Or look at Edinburgh itself. Who is it that gives the name to your own romantic town? It is no Celtic chief — it is no descendant of Fergus or Fingal. It is the Northumbrian Edwin, the first-fruits of Christian Yorkshire — the convert of the first English Primate of the North. And not only on England, but on France also, did Scotland lean, often as on a broken reed, even from her earliest days, both of Church and State. In Ninian's education at the centre of French Christianity in Tours, we have a dim foreshadowing of that long connection which so deeply colored the language and the architecture of Scotland through so many ages, and which, even in our own day, by a subtle sympathy, seemed to draw the heart of the Scottish nation, in spite of every political and ecclesiastical difference, towards the fortunes of suffering France during the late war. But this adventitious influence was still more apparent in the period which we are now approaching. The ancient Church had, although transported from a distance, become by the eleventh century thoroughly national. It was a Celtic Church, planted by Celtic missionaries in a Celtic people.

It was the "Scotland" beyond the Irish Channel that gave its name and religion to the Scotland of Iona and Melrose. But the Mediæval Church was altogether a foreign intrusion, the more so from the fact that it found a preëxisting Church to modify and subdue, and that it was imposed by Teutonic settlers on a Celtic population.

As Iona indicates the purely Irish character of the Church of Columba, so the Queen's Ferry and St. Margaret's Hope represent the purely English character of the Scottish Church of the Middle Ages. As across the Hebridean sea from Ireland came the ship which bore the first fortunes of Scottish Christianity, so up the recess of the Frith of Forth from England came the ship which bore the second. I need not repeat the romantic tale, how Margaret, the Saxon Princess, and her companions,[1] flying from the Norman conquerors, were driven ashore by stress of weather in the quiet bay which now bears her name; how she toiled along the track towards the Celtic "fortress by the winding stream" where Malcolm with the Great Head was intrenched in the depth of his wooded glen; how he found her seated on the stone which still may be seen on that same road by which she approached Dunfermline; how he wooed and won her hand; how she, with the arts of continental civilization then just taking root in England, soothed and tamed her fierce husband; how, under her guiding influence, rose the Westminster of Scotland, Dunfermline Abbey, the resting-place of kings, which henceforth diverted to itself for many

St. Margaret.

1 The whole story of Margaret is well told by Principal Shairp of St. Andrew's in *Good Words*, August, 1867.

generations the glory which had hitherto belonged to Iona. There, beside Malcolm, at the east end of the church, her remains reposed. Thence, on the eve of the battle of Largs, it was believed by the Scots that the tombs of Dunfermline gave up their dead, and that there passed through its northern porch to "war against the might of Norway" a lofty and "blooming matron in royal attire, leading in her right hand a noble knight, refulgent in arms, with a crown on his head, and followed by three heroic warriors, like armed, and like crowned."[1] These were Margaret, and her consort, and her three sons, the founders of the Mediæval Church of Scotland. "What she began those three sons long continued — the meek Edgar, the fierce Alexander, the saintly David. Their aim was to assimilate the Scottish Church in all respects to the English."

English influences.

Melrose, Holyrood, Kelso, Newbattle, Aberbrothock, Kinloss, Dryburgh, Jedburgh, and half the sees of Scotland, were founded by the third of these sons, and all these were based on an English model. The constitution of Glasgow and Dunkeld was copied from Salisbury, of Elgin and Aberdeen from Lincoln, Dunfermline from Canterbury, Coldingham from Durham, Melrose and Dundrennan from Rievaulx, Dryburgh from Alnwick, and Paisley from Wenlock.[2]

St. David, like his mother, was in all his thoughts and views an Englishman. The Church which they thus erected was, to all intents and purposes, an English Church, in the place of the old Celtic Church of the Culdees.

1 *Quart. Rev.* lxxxv. p. 120.

2 *Quart. Rev.* lxxxv. 117; Burton, ii. 62, 64.

Perhaps the spot which most distinctly brings to light the transfer of the seat of Scottish ecclesiastical forms from the Celtic west to the Anglicized east is St. Andrew's. It is dimly shadowed forth in the migration of Kenneth with his sacred stone from Dunstaffnage to Scone. It is traced more closely in the steps by which the venerable sea-girt fastness rose to be the primatial throne of Scotland. The remnant of the old Culdee church on the extreme promontory of the Muckross, or Headland of the Wild Boar, has been long superseded by the vast adjacent pile of the metropolitan cathedral. That pile rests for its legendary basis on the relics of the new patron saint of Scotland, which St. Rule brought from Achaia in his sailless and oarless boat, but for its historical basis on the new growth of Norman and English influences which spread from Fifeshire over the whole of Lowland Scotland.

See of St. Andrew's.

So fully was the external origin of the national episcopate recognized, that the supreme jurisdiction over the Scottish bishops was vested partly in the Norwegian Archbishop of Drontheim, partly in the English Archbishop of York.[1] It was not till the best of the mediæval prelates of Scotland, Bishop Kennedy, had so illustrated the see of St. Andrew's by his statesmanship and his virtues, that this badge of the foreign extraction of the Scottish Church was finally rejected, and that in 1472 it received for the first time a native primate.[2]

But the gaunt skeleton of the cathedral of St. Andrew's — the storm-vexed, shattered castle, which

1 Robertson's *Statuta Ecclesiæ Scotianæ*, Pref. pp. cxi., cxii.

2 Grub, i. 377.

witnessed from without the execution of Wishart, and from within the murder of Beaton — hurries us to the close of the mediæval Episcopacy of Scotland.

The fall of the Mediæval Church.

The fall, the tremendous fall, of the work of Margaret and David well indicates, from another point of view, its extraneous origin. The beginning of its decline dates from the hour when the power of England over Scotland was broken on the field of Bannockburn. Then, when the English intrusive elements were driven back across the Border, the Scottish episcopate received its death-blow. In a double, in a treble sense this may be traced. Partly the spirit thus evoked rose, as we shall see,[1] against English interference. Partly, and by a more immediate result, the disorder into which the country was thrown, and the withdrawal of the civilizing influences of England, led by degrees to the hideous and disproportionate corruption which took possession of the Scottish hierarchy during the last two centuries of its existence. This is an all-sufficient explanation for the wild [2] and disproportionate violence with which, beyond any other country in Europe, Scotland carried out the work of the Reformation.

[1] See Lecture II.

[2] I would not be understood here to refer to the common belief of the indiscriminate destruction of sacred buildings. Such a destruction doubtless took place at Perth and St. Andrew's. But it was not general, and the ruins which most immediately and conspicuously strike the eye of an English traveller at Melrose, Dryburgh, Jedburgh, and Kelso, were not the work of Scottish fanatics, but of the Catholic English soldiers of Henry VIII. (see *Quart. Rev.* lxxv. 141–150). What is meant is the extreme antagonism to ancient usages, as set forth in Lecture II.

III. We have now reached the third stage of our progress, which begins at the point when this connection between the English and Scottish Churches was to be rent asunder, and when in the sixteenth century the new elements eventually were exploded, which formed what has been the purely National Church of Scotland. On this I shall enter hereafter; but for the present I still continue to track the struggle of Episcopacy and of the English connection with the native influences at work in Scotland itself.

The modern Episcopal Church.

All know the attempts of the Stuart Kings to revive Episcopacy after its interruption by the Reformation. On the one hand it is curious to observe how, like the Episcopate of Margaret and David, it was not of Scottish but of English growth. Archbishop Spottiswoode, from whom the episcopal succession under James VI. took its rise, was consecrated entirely by English hands in the private chapel of London House, and lies himself in Westminster Abbey. Archbishop Sharpe, from whom the second succession sprang, under Charles II., was equally the creation of English prelates in the same Abbey, in the Chapel of Henry VII.

Its English origin.

But, on the other hand, whether from policy or necessity, the whole settlement of modern Scottish Episcopacy was far more Presbyterian, far less Episcopal and Catholic, than in any country in Europe. Doubtless this was partly occasioned by the fact, that in England itself the sentiment towards Presbyterian Churches was far more generous and comprehensive in the century which followed the Reformation than it was in that which followed the

Restoration. The English Articles are so expressed as to include the recognition of Presbyterian ministers. The first English Act of Uniformity was passed with the expressed view of securing their services to the English Church. The first English Reformers, and the statesmen of Elizabeth, would have been astonished at any claim of exclusive sanctity for the Episcopal order.[1] But it was in Scotland that this mutual recognition was most apparent. John Knox had as little belief in the paramount and divine character of Presbyterianism as Cranmer had in the paramount and divine character of Episcopacy. So far from shunning connection with the English Church, he eagerly sought to fortify its friendly relations with the Church of Scotland: so far from regarding the contact with Prelacy as a soul-destroying abomination, almost his last signature, "with a dead hand but a glad heart,"[2] is subscribed beneath the name of the Archbishop of St. Andrew's. It was not Knox, but Andrew Melville,[3] who introduced into Scotland the divine right of Presbytery, the sister dogma of the divine right of Episcopacy, which Bancroft and Laud introduced into England. But even after the mutual charities of the first age of the Reformation had been thus contracted, in Scotland,

Its relations to Presbyterianism.

[1] See this well drawn out in Lord Macaulay's Correspondence with the Bishop of Exeter; and in Principal Tulloch's article on the English and Scottish Churches in the *Contemporary Review*, December, 1871.

[2] See the signature to David Fergusson's sermon on Sacrilege (*Tracts of David Fergusson*, p. 80). The sermon itself which is thus recommended is also a remarkable proof of Knox's moderation. Communicated to me by the kindness of Lord Neaves.

[3] Compare Sir H. M. Wellwood's *Life of Erskine*, p. 507.

the two systems in practice flourished in the closest contact with each other. The General Assembly, of which the constitution had been inspired by Andrew Melville, continued to sit side by side with the hierarchy of James VI.[1] The Episcopalian curates in Charles II.'s reign were under the Presbytery, the Kirk session, and the Synod, with the Bishop presiding.[2] The Confession of Faith held by the Episcopal Church of Scotland was not that of the Episcopal Church of England; it was substantially the same as the Confession of John Knox.[3] The Scottish Prayer-book (with one exception, that of the words of administering the Eucharistic elements) was not, as is often erroneously supposed by both sides, more Roman and less Protestant than the English, but in all essential points was more Protestant and less Roman. "Presbyter" was everywhere substituted for "Priest." The Apocryphal Lessons were omitted. The service for the Eucharist embodied the true Protestant doctrine of spiritual sacrifice in the very centre of the consecration prayer far more prominently than is the case in the present English Prayer-book.[4] The consecration[5] itself was according to the Anti-Prelatic, not the Prelatic view of the subject. In the Ordination Service, as appointed

1 Cunningham, ii. 18. Even in the very acts of hostility this joint authority was recognized. The deposition of the Bishops of Charles I. by the General Assembly of Glasgow in 1638 was recognized as an ecclesiastical act, depriving them not only of all civil, but of all spiritual authority. See the interesting memorandum of Joseph Robertson, published in the *Scottish Guardian* of February 1, 1872, p. 71.

2 Burton, i. 269.

3 Innes's *Law of Creeds in Scotland*, pp. 38, 639.

4 See this well brought out in Bunsen's *Christianity and Mankind*, ii. 184–186.

5 *Scottish Liturgies*, p. 109.

under James VI., there was a marked exclusion[1] from the Ordination of Priests of the questionable words which, according to many devout churchmen, both of that time and our own, are "the very essential words of conferring orders." There was no form at all for the ordination of Deacons.[2] The Scottish Bishops of James VI. were not reordained in England.[3] Even the Scottish bishops of Charles II.'s time,[4] though they submitted to the ceremony, did so, as we shall see, at the advice of Leighton, on the ground that all such matters were wholly indifferent, and with one exception they never insisted on reordaining Scottish ministers[5] who had received Presbyterian ordination. The Prayer-book throughout the time of James VI. and Charles II. was never publicly used, except during the short time that the Princess Anne was with her father in Edinburgh.[6] The Episcopalian clergy and bishops preached and officiated in no peculiar dress, or else generally in black gowns, as distinct from the blue gowns and broad blue bonnets of the Presbyterians. This is the real origin of "Black Prelacy" and "True Blue Presbyterianism."[7] There was an Episcopal chapel in Forfarshire, where till quite recently the clergyman always officiated in black, and black serge was the only ecclesiastical vestment known at the beginning of this century in the Episcopal Church of Glasgow.

1 It seems that perhaps the omission was corrected under Charles I. *Scottish Liturgies*, p. lix.

2 Grub, ii. 322–324, 368.

3 Ibid. ii. 296.

4 Ibid. iii. 128. Tillotson was ordained priest by one of these bishops, who himself, though he had received episcopal consecration, had never received episcopal ordination.

5 Grub, iii. 218; see Lecture III.

6 Cunningham, ii. 250.

7 I owe this to the kindness of Dr. Crawfurd of Edinburgh.

The Communion was received sitting. The sign of the cross was not used in baptism. Extemporaneous instead of liturgical prayers were almost everywhere used. The requirement of tokens for the Eucharist, which was enjoined in the Scottish Prayer-book, is still in force in the Presbyterian Church, as well as in the older Episcopalian congregations of the north. In short, of all that now constitutes to the outward eye the main characteristics of Scottish Episcopacy, not one existed before the beginning of the eighteenth century.[1] The Episcopalian clergy, after the Revolution, were quite willing to officiate in manses and churches side by side with their Presbyterian brethren.[2] The nearly equal division of the country between them at that time, and the near approximation to an arrangement which might have included both within the same Church, and which would probably have succeeded but for purely political difficulties,[3] show how superficial after all were the differences which parted them. The earliest examples of the intrusion[4] of pastors by imperious patrons on unwilling congregations were not of Episcopalian or even Erastian incumbents on Presbyterian congregations, but of Presbyterian pastors on Episcopalian congregations.

Its state of persecution.

There remains to be considered the final aspect of the Episcopal Church, when it was proscribed in its turn as it had itself proscribed the Covenanters. In one sense, indeed, it has never entirely lost its legal position. It was, and is still

[1] Burton, viii. 467.

[2] Leighton, as we shall see, was Presbyterian by ordination; Rutherford may have been, perhaps was, Episcopalian by ordination. See the case argued in *Life of Rutherford*, p. 38.

[3] Grub, iii. 311–318.

[4] Burton, viii. 220.

entitled the "Episcopal Communion, protected and allowed by an Act passed in the tenth year of the reign of Queen Anne, chapter seven." In later years it received a small state endowment, only recently withdrawn from it. But during and after the Stuart Rebellion, it was visited by a hand almost as heavy as that which had rested on the Presbyterians at the close of the preceding century; and it is a salutary warning to mutual forbearance when we read the very same adventures in the very same caves and moss hags — the very same apprehension of the lapwings hovering near the place of their concealment, as had breathed through the legends of the Cameronians.[1]

From necessity, as well as from inclination, more and more the Episcopal communion shrank from its public place in the nation, except in the short periods when the Stuart Princes were for the moment in the ascendant. Carubbers Close was their metropolitan church. "I have been looking," said Dundee, "for the primate of the Episcopal Church, and cannot find him; he belongs to the Kirk Invisible." "I belong," says Pleydell in "Guy Mannering," "to the suffering Episcopal Church of Scotland, which is now — happily — the shadow of a shade."[2]

But there are three points during this dark and secluded period in which it was still thoroughly Scottish and thoroughly national.

First, it shared to the full that peculiarity of Scottish religion which will appear most distinctly in my next lecture, — its violent divisions

1. Its violent divisions.

[1] Lord Medwyn's *Life of Lord Pitsligo*, p. 32.

[2] In 1745 there were not more than 150 clergy in communion with the Scottish bishops. Grub, iv. 32.

on points of the smallest dimensions. What Burghers and Anti-Burghers, Relief and Secession, Old and New Lights were to the followers of John Knox, that the long disputes of Collegers[1] and Usagers, of old Episcopalians and new Episcopalians, of the Scottish and the English Communion Offices, often were to the followers of Laud and Sharpe. No ecclesiastical struggle, except that of the rival Popes, has more tried the Episcopal system than that in the month of June, 1727, in Edinburgh, when the bishops of the two contending parties of Collegers and Usagers strove to outdo each other by consecrating and deposing rival bishops, so as to secure the point at issue, "if not by equal arguments, yet by equal numbers.[2]

2. Antagonism to the English Church and State.

Secondly, there was the antagonism to the English Church and State. This, which in the Puritans was produced by the hostility to a government which rejected the Covenant, in the Episcopalians was produced by the hostility to a government which rejected the divine hereditary right of kings.

In the time of the Stuart sovereigns, the Episcopalians of Scotland were almost as Erastian as their English brethren. But this gradually passed away; the anti-Hanoverian tendencies of the Episcopal clergy gradually detached them from their ancient principles; and the "Usagers" went to the length of throwing aside their loyalty to King James, for which their brethren the "Collegers" were ready to sacrifice everything. To a certain degree this feeling has lasted almost to our own day. The memory of

1 See Grub, iii. 387; iv. 21–29.

2 Skinner, ii. 644, 645. Cunningham, ii. 398. Grub, iv. 5, 6.

the massacre of Glencoe still lives in the Episcopalian inhabitants of the fatal valley, when it has expired elsewhere. Jacobitism and not Liberalism was and is the root of the Episcopalian jealousy of state interference.[1] It was with the utmost reluctance that, in the last century, the Scottish Episcopalians could be induced to accept the English Articles,[2] or to hear the name of George III. in the English Liturgy; and no Presbyterians could have been more alarmed than they were at the encroachments of the English clergy.[3] One of the solemn articles of agreement with the American bishop of Connecticut was, that the members of his church, when in Scotland, should hold no communion in sacred offices with those "persons who, under the pretense of ordination by an English or an Irish bishop, do, or shall take upon them to officiate as clergymen in any part of the national Church of Scotland, and whom the Scottish bishops cannot help looking upon as schismatical[4] intruders."

3. Its romance.

This leads me to the third characteristic, which has found its home more completely in the Scottish Episcopalians than in any other of the Church of Scotland more strictly so called, when, from being an aspiring or a dominant Church, it became a vanquished and persecuted communion; when, for its attachment to the exiled Stuarts, it became the Church of the Jacobites and Nonjurors.

1 It was not without reason that when a celebrated English divine wished to express his covert hostility to the doctrine of the connection of Church and State, he did so under the assumed name of "a Scottish Episcopalian." The effect of these "Letters" in determining the future theological career of Dr. Newman is powerfully described in his "Apologia," p. 70.

2 Grub, iv. 101, 115.

3 Ibid. iv. 174.

4 Ibid. iv. 94.

No history of any European state has been so romantic as that of Scotland. Whatever England has to show of early romance pales before the stories of Robert Bruce and James V. What English abbey can in this respect compete with Melrose? what chapel with Rosslyn? what city with Edinburgh? What are the earliest efforts of English poetry— what are the triads of Wales, or the early songs of Ireland, compared with the romantic charm (whatever be their other merits or demerits) of the poems of Ossian? It is this peculiar embodiment of Scottish character that Shakespeare has reproduced in "Macbeth." Whether or not he was in that band of actors who came to amuse King James VI. at Aberdeen, it is certain that he has caught the general air and tone of Scottish scenery and Scottish history: the blasted heath, extending for leagues along the coast of Forres; the witches lingering in Scotland long after they had died out in the rest of Europe; the castles, haunted by deeds of blood, and by dead men's ghosts; the prophetic dooms of royal families and great houses; this is the very genius of Scotland, because it belongs to that weird, uncanny, magic world which has always enveloped Scotland as in a mist of wonders. And when that "meet Nurse for a poetic child" produced a second Shakespeare of her own, this was the atmosphere in which he was born and bred. Walter Scott had many greater qualities, which I shall describe before I conclude these lectures; but it was this "wizard note" of the mediæval past, with all its spells and glamours, that first woke "the Harp of the North" to its special task.

It is this element of which so large a share is reflected in the modern Episcopalian Church of Scotland. There are three great historic names which specially represent this passion, and which all belong to the stream of Episcopalian tradition. One is Mary Queen of Scots. Hers is a story which has become thoroughly national, yet certainly not Presbyterian — not even Protestant. To John Knox and Andrew Melville the name of the ill-fated Queen suggests the idea of a perfidious and abandoned murderess. It is by the ancient Catholic, by the modern Episcopalian party in Scotland, that the fire of veneration for the unfortunate Mary has been kept alive. The next is Dundee.[1] The interest which gathers round the last exploits of Claverhouse — which glorifies the Pass of Killikrankie, and which has enkindled all the fury of chivalrous defense in his behalf, even within our own time, is purely and exclusively Episcopalian. He is the hero of the fallen cause. He was lamented by the Episcopalian party as the last of the Grahams, the last of the Scots, the last (in their eyes) of all that was greatest in his native country.[2] The third is Charles Edward. His career is not only the last great romance of Scotland, it is almost the last romance of Europe. Round his name — round his career — cling the last traditions of Highland fidelity, of mediæval adventure, of soul-stirring ballad; and they were interwoven with the innermost fibres of the Scottish Episcopal Church in the eighteenth century.

No doubt each of these is but a questionable idol.

[1] He is said to have been the first intelligent admirer of Ossian. Burton, viii. 104.

[2] Scott, *History of Scotland*, ii. 115.

The church which worshipped at the shrine of Mary Stuart, of Claverhouse, and of Charles Edward, could hardly be said to have reached the highest ideal of Christian excellence. In the whole Stuart and Jacobite cause there was (as every reader of "Waverley" may see) a worldly, weak, and trivial side. But there was also a noble, a chivalrous, a poetic side; and of this the Episcopalian gentry and the Episcopalian clergy were the chief depositaries.[1] Who that had ever seen the delightful castle of Fingask, explored its inexhaustible collection of Jacobite relics, known its Jacobite inmates, and heard its Jacobite songs, did not feel himself transported to an older world, with the fond remembrance of a past age, of a lost love, of a dear though vanquished cause? Who is the Scotsman — who is the Presbyterian that is not moved by the outburst of Jacobite, Episcopalian enthusiasm which enkindled the last flicker of expiring genius, when Walter Scott murmured the lay of Prince Charlie on the hills of Pausilippo, and stood wrapped in silent devotion[2] before the tomb of the Stuarts in St. Peter.

Let me, in parting from this period of Scottish history, take two examples of its peculiar fruits. No church is worth celebrating which has not borne some choice manifestation of the Christian life. Every church, however limited, is worth describing, which has borne any such as, humanly speaking, we should not have had but for its influence.

One is a layman, Alexander Forbes — Lord Pit-

[1] Let me also name, in connection with these same subjects, the noble band of Scottish antiquaries living and dead, some of the most distinguished of whom have have been Episcopalians.

[2] See Lord Houghton's Poems.

sligo. If, as I have heard it said, he is the original of the "Baron of Bradwardine," he is sufficiently known to all the world. But we cannot imagine a more gracious and attractive specimen of that type of character of which I have been speaking, than is presented to us in the little volume published by his kinsman, Lord Medwyn. His hair-breadth escapes I leave to be read in those pages. But his kindly, generous feeling towards his opponents, the mystical piety which he had learned in France from Fénelon and Madame Guyon, the unostentatious sincerity which made his presence at the Episcopal chapel the signal for a general sympathy of devotion, are the true glory of the Episcopal Church of that time. When, in spite of his age and infirmities, he determined to join Charles Edward at Aberdeen, he believed that he was simply obeying the call of God. When the little party of horsemen assembled, he rode to the front, took off his hat, and, looking up to heaven, said, "Lord, Thou knowest our cause is just. March, gentlemen." "It seemed," says one who was present when he joined the army, "as if religion, virtue, and justice were entering the camp with this venerable old man."[1]

Lord Pitsligo.

If Lord Pitsligo may be taken as a choice specimen of the old Episcopalian laity, Bishop Jolly may be taken as a choice specimen of the old Episcopalian clergy. He was a man, of whom it was wittily observed by one of his abler and younger brethren still living, "that he had a reason for nothing, and an authority for everything;" who, when he was asked at the beginning of the stir oc-

Bishop Jolly.

[1] Grub, iv. 190.

casioned by the Oxford Tracts, what he thought of the Reformation, said that "he had not come down so far in his regular course of Ecclesiastical history." "You go," said an American traveller, "from the extremity of Britain to see the Falls of Niagara, and think yourselves amply rewarded. If I had come from America to Aberdeen, and seen nothing but Bishop Jolly, as I saw him for two days, I should hold myself fully rewarded. In our new country we have no such men; and I could not have imagined such without seeing him. The race, I fear, is expired or expiring even among you." His departure was like his life. The last book which he held in his hand on the evening before his death, was Sutton's treatise, "Disce Mori;" and he was found, alone, with his hands crossed on his breast, and his countenance serene in death.

Doubtless the primitive simplicity, the gentleness, the quiet retiring holiness which so struck the transatlantic traveller in the aged bishop, was shared by many others in the Episcopalian households of Scotland high and low. Perhaps of this whole type of character it may be said, that it is expired or expiring. But it was a precious and peculiar spectacle in those rough rude times; it is for us at least to cherish the memory of it.

IV. These, then, were some of the latest peculiarities of the Episcopal Church of Scotland in the century that is gone. I would venture to say a few words on its peculiarity, rather, let me say, its peculiar mission, in this. It has ceased to be half Presbyterian, as it was in the seventeenth century. It has ceased to be Jacobite, as it was in the eighteenth.

It is now, for the most part, and for practical purposes, a branch of the English Church in Scotland; for the benefit of the English settlers, or of Scotsmen with an English education. Native congregations of Episcopalians doubtless exist, the descendants of those Jacobites and Nonjurors of whom I have just spoken. Individuals have migrated from Scottish Presbyterian families, under the changed circumstances of later times. But the larger section of the Scottish Episcopal communion derive their importance from the new influences that I have indicated, and from the connection, once so much dreaded, but now so much encouraged, between themselves and the Church of England.

In this, as we have seen, lies the true continuity of its connection with the historical past; in this lies its interest in the coming future. The increased intercourse between the two countries has increased and fostered its strength, its numbers, and its wealth. If it were so ill-advised as to make use of this its new situation to claim in Scotland an exclusive and national position; if it were to affect to disdain and ignore the Church of Scotland, by the side of which it has been allowed freely to expand itself; if it were to employ its relations towards England to divide the Scottish rich from the Scottish poor, the past from the present history of Scottish religion; if it were to lend itself as a field for the eccentricities of[1] disaffected English clergy, then, indeed, we might look back with regret to the time when the greatest of its members rejoiced to think that it was "but

[1] It was but fair to say that on the two chief occasions when this attempt was made, it was frustrated by the leaders of the Episcopal Church itself.

the shadow of a shade." But if, following the counsels[1] of its most venerable and most gifted leaders, it were to regard itself as a supplement to the needs of the National Church; if it should be willing "to interchange with that Church all good offices, whether of charity or religion, without compromise of its own principles;" if it should aid the generous efforts of the National Church to promote that intercourse; if it should thus encourage in Scotland the knowledge that Christianity can exist outside of the Presbyterian Church, as well as within it; if it can keep alive in Scotland, by its own example, a sense of English art, of English toleration, and of English literature; if it continued to discharge the office which from time to time it has fulfilled during its simpler and humbler days, of presenting Christian life and Christian truth under that softer, gentler, more refined aspect, which its native Gaelic,[2] and its foreign English elements have alike conspired to produce, then the Church of Scotland may hail in it a not unimportant auxiliary for the transmission of the same beneficent influences from our southern civilization that were once conveyed by Queen Margaret and her three sons, that were eagerly cherished by John Knox, and that were desired and, in great measure obtained, by the eminent statesmen who cemented the union of the two Kingdoms.

1 See especially the close of the 20th edition of *Reminiscences of Scottish Life and Character*, by Dean Ramsay, pp. 320–325.

2 For this singular delicacy of the old Celtic race, see Bishop Ewing's *Celtic Church of the West Highlands*, p. 8.

LECTURE II.

THE CHURCH OF SCOTLAND, THE COVENANT, AND THE SECEDING CHURCHES.

DELIVERED BEFORE THE PHILOSOPHICAL INSTITUTE,

JANUARY 9, 1872.

LECTURE II.

THE CHURCH OF SCOTLAND, THE COVENANT, AND THE SECEDING CHURCHES.

In this and the ensuing lectures I proceed to speak of the Church of Scotland, properly so called. In the mouth of an English Churchman, no less than of an impartial historian, I need not say that this can only mean the Church as established by law. It is this for which every English Churchman is asked to pray, by the canons of the English Convocation, which enjoin that prayers are to be offered up "for Christ's Holy Catholic Church, that is, for the whole congregation of Christians dispersed throughout the world, especially for the Churches of England, *Scotland*, and Ireland." "There can be no doubt," says the candid and accurate annalist of Scottish Episcopacy, "that the framers of this have meant to acknowledge the northern ecclesiastical establishment, at that time Presbyterian, as a Christian Church. . . . . With the exception of the Roman Catholics, it was the only Christian communion then existing in Scotland, and questions regarding any other state of matters than that actually before them could not have occurred to the Convocation."[1] It is this also which is recognized in the most solemn form by the British Constitution.

The Church of Scotland is the National Established Church.

[1] See the discussion on the Canons of 1603 in Grub, ii. 282.

The very first declaration which the sovereign makes—taking precedence even of the recognition of the rights and liberties of the English Church and nation, which are postponed till the day of the coronation—is that in which, on the day of the accession, the sovereign declares that he or she will maintain inviolate and intact the Church of Scotland. That which was signed by her Majesty may be seen in the Register House of Edinburgh, and has the peculiar interest of being the first signature of her name as Queen. There is a large blank left, in the doubt which was then not yet solved, whether one or more of her names would be used, and the single name therefore stands—alone of all her signatures—in a space too ample for the word; and immediately following comes, after the signature of the Princes of the Blood Royal, the name of the dignified and cautious Primate who then filled the see of Canterbury. In the Act of Union itself, which prescribes this declaration, the same securities are throughout exacted for the Church of Scotland as were exacted for the Church of England; and it is on record that, when that act was passed, and some question arose amongst the Peers as to the propriety of so complete a recognition of the Presbyterian Church, the then Primate of all England, the "old rock," as he was called, Archbishop Tenison, rose, and said with a weight which carried all objections before it, "The narrow notions of all churches have been their ruin. I believe that the Church of Scotland, though not so perfect as ours, is as true a Protestant Church as the Church of England." [1]

[1] Carstairs' *State Papers*, 739, 760.

No Scotsman, no Englishman can see the meeting of the General Assembly in Edinburgh without feeling that it is the chief national institution of the northern kingdom. No other ecclesiastical assembly in the realm meets with such a solemn and distinct recognition, with such a pomp and circumstance of royalty, with such a well-ordered and well-understood tradition of rights and privileges and duties.

What is thus legally acknowledged receives a yet further confirmation in the common parlance even of unwilling witnesses. It is sometimes the custom of English Churchmen and Scottish Episcopalians, to distinguish in Scotland between "the Church" and "the Kirk," meaning by the former the Episcopalian, and by the latter the Presbyterian system. It is difficult to imagine a more complete testimony to the national character of the Presbyterian Church than this surrender to it of the true Scottish name of the Church itself. The "Kirk," whatever the word may mean in English, in Scotland means "the Church" as truly as *Église* in French, or *Chiesa* in Italian. To speak of the Presbyterian community as "the Kirk," and the Episcopalian community as "the Church," is in fact to say that the Presbyterian community is the national Church of Scotland, and the Episcopalian community an offshoot of the Church of England.

I shall therefore not hesitate to speak of "the Church of Scotland" in its more peculiar and proper sense, as that which, under divers changes, has settled down into the great Presbyterian Church of North Britain.

I have, however, already intimated, that I thus use

the word the more readily because, in a certain sense, it embraces all the various branches into which it has at times been divided, and because, in so speaking, we are brought face to face with one of the most singular features of the Scottish Presbyterian Church, namely, its marvelous outward uniformity. The Church of England, no doubt, in the largest legal sense, includes alike all Englishmen, whether conforming or non-conforming; but whereas in England every branch of the vast religious community, so called, has its own peculiar constitution — and the Convocation, the Thirty-nine Articles, the Prayer-book of the Established Church; the Conference of the Wesleyans, with its "Conferential" books; the Congregational Union of the Independents; the monthly meetings of the Quakers; — whereas, even in the Established Church, the ritual, in spite of the Act of Uniformity, varies from the majestic splendor of St. Paul's Cathedral to the elaborate ceremonial of St. Alban's, Holborn, and the simplicity of the ordinary parish church — in Scotland, on the other hand, with very rare exceptions, all the Presbyterian communions acknowledge not only the same Westminster Confession, the same Directory, the same Longer and Shorter Catechisms, but also the same form of Presbytery, Kirk Session, and General Assembly, the same dress, the same order of Divine worship, the same gestures in prayer and praise, the same form in the sacramental ordinances, the same observances at the burial of the dead. It is a uniformity which Rome might have enjoined, and which England might envy.

Its unity.

But, combined with this phenomenon, emerges the

not less curious and instructive fact that, within this outward unity has arisen an amount of inward diversity and estrangement which England, with her multifarious sects, and even Rome, with the internecine war of her internal dissensions, can hardly equal or surpass. This is a fact which, under any circumstances, is full of interest.

Its divisions.

Every Church, whether Catholic or Protestant, may always learn a useful lesson from the contemplation of any instance which brings out the essential difference between external and dogmatic union on the one side, and inward spiritual union on the other side. The Church of Scotland is, in this respect, like a city set on a hill for the wonder of all the churches of Europe, even before we descend into the causes and consequences of the phenomenon. It is this task which we now undertake.

The general fact is that, within the National Church of Scotland, as within the character of the Scottish people, there are two separate tendencies: one of an uniting, comprehensive character, which I shall consider at length in my third lecture; the other of a dividing, antagonistic character, of which I shall treat in the present.

It will be my object, therefore, to penetrate beneath the surface of the Presbyterian platform which the Scottish Church has in common with the Protestant Churches of Geneva, Holland, France, and Germany — to discover, if possible, those elements of the Scottish national character which form, as it were, the backbone of its ecclesiastical constitution, and which, though appearing from time to time in the Established, or even the Episcopalian Church, are best seen in those outlying sections which, claiming each to be the Church of Scotland, exhibit in the most salient, but therefore the most patent and unmistakable forms, the strength and the weakness of Scottish religion. As in speaking of Scottish Episcopacy, so in speaking of Scottish Presbyterianism, it will be understood that I dwell not on the general life and belief common to all Christian Churches alike, but on those peculiarities which distinguish each from each.

National independence.

I. The first feature then which marks the Scottish religion of the last three centuries is its stubborn independence.

When James VI. saw in London Mrs. Welsh, the daughter of John Knox, he asked her how many bairns her father had left, and whether they were lads or lasses. She answered "Three," and that they were all lasses. "God be thanked!" said the king, lifting up both his hands; "for if they had been three lads, I never could have brooked my three kingdoms in peace."[1]

The feeling of King James towards John Knox and his actual children may well have been felt at times by many reasonable men towards his spiritual children. Had each of the three kingdoms been inhabited by a Church as sturdy and as unmanageable as that which took up its abode in Scotland, it may be easily believed that the rulers of Great Britain would have had no light task before them.

This independence of the Scottish Church belongs in fact to the independence of the Scottish race. It was nurtured, if not produced, by the long struggle first of Wallace and then of Bruce, which gave to the

[1] Cunningham, ii. 43.

whole character of the people a defiant self-reliance, such as, perhaps, is equally impressed on no other kingdom in Europe. The patriotism and the ecclesiastical exclusiveness of Davie Deans in the "Heart of Midlothian," flow in the same indivisible channel. "Well, said that judicious Christian worthy, John Livingston . . . . that, howbeit he thought Scotland a Gehenna of wickedness when he was at home, yet when he was abroad he accounted it as a paradise. For the evils of Scotland he found everywhere, and the good of Scotland he found nowhere." And when Jeanie Deans shrinks from giving up the slayer of Porteous, it is because her religious education had made her regard it as an act of treason against the independence of Scotland. "With the fanaticism of the Scottish Presbyterians there was always mingled a glow of national feeling, and she trembled at the idea of her name being handed down to posterity with that of the 'fause Menteith.'" Burns's imaginary address of Bruce at Banockburn is but the counterpart of the genuine song of the Covenanters at Dunselaw: —

"That all the warld may see
There 's nane in the right but we,
Of the auld Scottish nation."

The badge of the Church of Scotland — the Burning Bush, "burning but not consumed" — is as true a type of Scotland's inexpugnable defense of her ancient liberties, as it was of the ancient Jewish Church and people on their emergence from Egyptian bondage. And so the early history of the Scottish Presbyterian Church has been one long struggle of dogged resistance to superior power. "Scotland must be rid of Scotland, unless we gain deliverance," was the dying speech of the martyr Renwick.[1]

Many of the Scottish sects have in later times drifted into the doctrine of an imaginary separation from the state and nation. Nothing can be more unjust to themselves, or more untrue to history. Their independence is as secular, as political, as national as ever was the compliance of the most latitudinarian of Erastians. It is this antique splendor which casts a halo round the Scottish struggle for independence, even when we least approve of it. It was magnificent in the struggle of John Knox against all the fascinations of Queen Mary. It was magnificent in the struggle of Andrew Melville against James VI. It was magnificent, even if somewhat grotesque, in the struggle of the whole people against Laud and Charles I. It was magnificent in the still more fiery struggle of the Covenanters against Claverhouse and Lauderdale. It was magnificent when, passing over into the Episcopalian Church, it strove against William III. at Killikrankie, or against George II. at Prestonpans and Culloden. It magnificently combined both the extreme Episcopalians and the extreme Presbyterians in its unavailing[2] protests against the endeavors of the wisest statesmen of England and Scotland to bring about the union of the two countries. It was magnificent even when carried to a pitch of extravagance of dissent unequaled by any other nation in the various entrenchments occupied by the Cove-

[1] Wodrow.

[2] See the lively description of this opposition in the brilliant lecture on "The Union," with which the course of lectures at the Philosophical Institute, in 1871, was opened by Lord Rosebery.

nanters, by the Secession, by the Relief, by the Old Lights, by the New Lights, by the Collegers, by the Usagers, by the Burghers, by the Anti-burghers, by the Free Church, and by the United Presbyterians, against the Established Church, and against each other, in every one of the contests in which each separating communion maintained that it, and it alone, was the true Church of Scotland.

The main peculiarity of dissent in Scotland has been that it was not properly dissent at all, and that it earnestly repudiated the name. English Nonconformists pride themselves on their nonconformity; but Scottish Nonconformists pride themselves on their churchmanship. In this respect they are like the Dissenters of Russia. They are, indeed, with the exception of the Russian Dissenters, the most conservative of all ecclesiastical bodies.[1] They looked not forward to an age of progress, but backward to a golden age of purity — the triumphant Church from 1636 to 1680. Their claim of identity with the doctrine, discipline, and worship of the Church of Scotland was the very cause of their separation. They seceded not from the Church itself, but from the majorities of the Church, "out of a regard to the Church's honor and faithfulness; and their bitterness was the perverted flow of love."[2]

By one of those strange contradictions which we often find in ecclesiastical and political movements, these elements, which in their own nature are in the highest degree retrogressive and conservative, have become mixed up with what is called a Liberal

1 *Lectures on the Eastern Church.* Lecture XII.

2 Innes's *Law of Creeds in Scotland*, p. 246.

movement; and the cause which has for its watchwords the names of Freedom and Progress, has for its weapons the sword and shield of the narrowest of all beliefs, and the most retrograde of all philosophies. Yet there still lives at the bottom of this tendency of the Scottish character a virtue, most highly to be valued, most necessary for these times especially, whether in the ranks of Conservatives or Liberals; and that is the force of unyielding conviction, the courage to resist external pressure, whether of the many or of the few; the determination of James Fitz-James: —

> "Come one, come all — this rock shall fly
> From its firm base as soon as I."

All honor to Scottish Churchmen for the stubbornness of their fight, their devotion not only of themselves to death, but, at times, even to absurdity, for what were deemed the rights of conscience, and the sacredness of truth, and the glory of Scotland.

When we descend from the general grandeur of the cause to the principles at stake, the story, if less imposing, is still exceedingly instructive.

Negative character.

1. There are three features of these Scottish ecclesiastical struggles which pervade their whole history. The first is their almost entirely negative character. We often hear, in modern times, of the evils of negative theology. It is an objection which is sometimes overstrained, for in order to promote truth we must remove error, and every removal of error is a negation. Still, whether for good or evil, no church has so abounded in purely negative theology as the Scottish. It is the only Church which produced by name a "Negative

Confession of Faith,"[1] containing only the doctrines which were not to be believed, instead of the doctrines which are to be believed. In order to see any likeness to it we must go back to the Fourth Council of Toledo, and study the creed of the Visigothic King Reccared, which consists from first to last of nothing but anathemas.[2] It is the only Protestant Church which has even amongst its more temperate forms of subscription not only assertions of truths to be embraced, but an enumeration of errors to be condemned. "Do you disown all Popish, Arian, Socinian, Arminian, Bourignian,[3] and other doctrines, tenets, and opinions whatever, contrary to and inconsistent with the Confession of Faith?" It is the only Church which could boast of a branch professing to be the purest section of the Church, known by the simple and convenient name of *No.* The Presbyterian *Non*-Jurors were for many years characteristically and gravely designated by the simple name of *Nons.*[4] The "dying testimonies," as well as the living creed, of this purest of Presbyterian Churches were all couched in this uniformly antagonistic form.

"I leave my protest," says a stern Cameronian, in the middle of the last century, "against all sectarian errors, heresies, and blasphemies, particularly against Arianism, Erastianism, Socinianism, Quakerism, Deism, Bourignianism, Familism, Skepticism, Arminian-

1 The name given to the "National Covenant" of 1850. Innes's *Law of Creeds*, p. 36. Cunningham, i. 448.

2 Harduin's *Councils*, iii. 473.

3 The denunciation of the innocent Antonia Bourignon, which was the last added (Cunningham, ii. 325), has been the first dropped. The rigid Free Church, in this respect alone freer than the Established, allows of the orthodoxy of this good, though eccentric, French lady who taught it.

4 Burton, ix. 60.

ism, Lutheranism, Brownism, Baxterianism, Anabaptism, Millenarianism, Pelagianism, Campbellianism, Whitfieldianism, Latitudinarianism, and Independency, and all other sects and sorts that maintain any error, heresy, or blasphemy that is contrary to the Word of God, etc., and all erroneous speeches vented from pulpits, pages, or in public or private discourses; and against all toleration granted or given at any time, in favor of these or any other errors, heresies, or blasphemies, or blasphemous heretics, particularly the toleration granted by the sectarian usurper, Oliver Cromwell, the anti-Christian toleration granted by the Popish Duke of York, and the present continued toleration granted by that wicked Jezebel, the pretended Queen Anne."[1]

And this negation is carried out even into the details of Ritual. Scotland, as well as England, has its Ritualism, its symbolism. But its symbolism is one which depends for its meaning not on what it affirms but on what it rejects. The Church of Scotland sat in praise, because others stood. It stood in prayer because others knelt. It was silent in funerals because others spoke. It repudiated Christmas because others observed it. I do not say that this symbolism is not as reasonable or as edifying as much that we cherish beyond the Border; but it is a symbolism peculiar to Scotland, and originating in that antagonism of which I have spoken.

Negation, as I have said, has its value, and has its drawbacks. The Church of Scotland, in the aspect which we are now considering, is a splendid specimen both of the good and evil of this form of theol-

[1] Burton, ix. 60.

ogy. There is a sentence of Voltaire which well illustrates its use, "That which resists supports." Such has been the beneficent side of the contradictious character of the Scottish Church. There is a sentence of Goethe which describes how the scoffing Fiend is always saying "No" and never "Yes." That is the darker side even of the most fervent forms of the same tendency.

The second feature is the vigor which has been given to the claims of spiritual independence. It is extremely difficult to distinguish how far this is a development of the passion for national independence, and of the passion of antagonism already mentioned; or how far it has a separate ecclesiastical growth. It can hardly be doubted that, in the first instance, if not created it was greatly fostered by the historical circumstances of the formation of the Scottish Church. The original independence of the General Assembly was an accident arising from the political confusion of Scotland at the time. It soon received the sanction of the legislature, which at once placed it in a unique position amongst Protestant Churches. What was called its spiritual authority was, in fact, temporal power conceded on a very large scale to a body which became the Second Parliament of Scotland. This claim to independence from the state was, in the close of the seventeenth century, increased from another quarter. The original Covenanters, so far from being opposed to interference of the civil power in ecclesiastical affairs, laid it down as one of the fundamental maxims of their Solemn League, that the state should be bound to promote true religion, and to procure that all

Spiritual independence.

"evil instruments for hindering the reformation of religion shall receive condign punishment from the supreme judicatories of the kingdom." The "new forcers of Conscience" under the Long Parliament, whom Milton attacked with such unsparing vehemence, were the leaders of the Covenant. It was they

"Who dared adjure the civil sword
To force the consciences which Christ set free;
Taught them by mere A. S. and Rutherford,
To ride us with a classic hierarchy."

But when the State had broken loose from the Covenant, the Covenanting section of the Church in retaliation broke loose from the State; and the protest in behalf of Christ's "kingly rights," as the doctrine was called, though in its ideal sense intended to assert the true doctrine of the supremacy of duty and religion over every other consideration, drifted away into the secondary and very subordinate question of the supremacy of the Covenanting Church over the Uncovenanted State; and thence, as the traditions of the Covenant faded away, into the yet more remote and subordinate position of the supremacy of ecclesiastical courts, whether covenanted or uncovenanted, over all civil courts whatever. "We never," says Ralph Erskine, "declared a secession from the Church of Scotland, but only a secession from the judicatories in their course of defection from the primitive and covenanted constitution." [1]

Out of these converging circumstances, combined with the more democratic spirit of the Scottish people, much more than from any fixed or abstract principle, sprung those claims of spiritual indepen-

[1] Phillips's *Whitefield*, p. 231.

dence which have been raised within the Church of Scotland, in a stronger form than in any Christian community, except that of Rome; and which, though they reached their highest form in the Cameronians and in the Free Church, exist in a modified shape both in the Established Church and in the Episcopal[1] communion. Out of these tendencies grew that extreme sensitiveness of the Scottish clergy to regal or legislative interference, which Hallam well calls "Presbyterian Hildebrandism,"[2] which has caused the name "Erastian" to be placed in the blackest list of heresies.

The doctrine is no doubt a representation, greatly distorted, of a noble truth—the indefeasible superiority of moral over material force—of conscience over power—of right against might, and the vehemence with which it was supported in Scotland gave a strong impulse to the cause of Civil Liberty. But this heavenly treasure has been often enshrined in very earthly vessels; and in its earthly as well as its nobler aspects it has curiously brought into close proximity the two churches which naturally are most opposed to each other. Hildebrand and Andrew Melville would doubtless have started with horror at either being thought the twin-brother of the other. But so it was; and even in actual history the affinity has been recognized. Walter Scott has finely touched a living chord when he described how Balfour of Burley at last made common cause with the Episcopalian Claverhouse against the English invaders; and, in our own time, the admiration excited amongst English High Churchmen by the Disruption of 1843

1 See Lecture I. 2 *Constitutional History of England*, iii. 421.

led by rapid steps to their own large secession to the Roman Church in 1845; and the most estimable of Scottish Free Churchmen has found a welcome ally in the most prelatical of Anglican colonial bishops.

There are two well known scenes which bring out clearly the form in which these feelings of antagonism and independence displayed themselves.

Rejection of the English Liturgy.

The rejection of the English Liturgy took place on July 23, 1637. There is an exact forecast of these troubles so descriptive of Scottish religion, and so much to the credit of the good sense and good faith, perhaps, one may add, the Scottish prudence of James VI., that even if open to question as to some of its details, it is worth citing both as a prelude and a comment. "I keep him back," said the King (speaking of Laud, not yet Archbishop), "because he hath a restless spirit. When, three years since, I had obtained from the Assembly of Perth the consent to the Five Articles of order and decency in correspondence with the Church of England, I gave the promise that I would try their obedience no further anent ecclesiastical affairs, yet this man hath pressed me to incite them to a nearer conjunction with the Liturgy and Canons of England; but I sent him back again with the previous draft he had drawn. . . . . For all this he feared not mine anger, but assaulted me again with another ill-fangled platform to *make that stubborn kirk stoop* more to the English pattern. But I durst not play fast and loose with my soul. *He* knows not the stomach of that people. But *I* ken the story of my grandmother, the Queen Margaret, that after she was inveigled to break her promise made to some mutineers at a Perth meeting, she never saw good-day, but from thence, being much beloved before, was despised of all the people."[1]

What the result was in St. Giles's Church on that fatal day, when the "black, popish, and superstitious book," as it was called, was opened by the unfortunate Dean of Edinburgh, can hardly be imagined in these more peaceful days. "Wolf," "crafty fox," "son of a witch," "false Judas," were the epithets with which the prelates who assisted were "mightily upbraided;" and, had they been actually all these things, they could hardly have been worse treated. And yet, "these speeches" of a certain woman, says a grave eyewitness, "proceeded not" (and probably he was quite right) "from any particular savage or inveterate malice that could be conceived against the Bishop's person, but only from a zeal to God's glory, wherewith the woman's heart was burnt up; for, had she not discerned the signs of the beast in the Bishop's bowels of conformity, she had[2] never set against him with such a sharp-tongued assault."

The two special incidents, which figure in all versions of the tumult, under different forms, deserve a more particular notice.

The first was when "the old herb-woman" "hearing the Archbishop, who watched the rubric, direct the Dean to read the Collect of the day," gathered up her indignation in the well known exclamation, confounding "cholic" and "collect," and discharged at the Dean's head the famous stool, which he escaped by "jowking," but gave the signal for a universal discharge of the like fauld stools of the

1 Hacket's *Williams*, p. 14. 2 *Appendix to Lord Rothes*, p. 200.

ladies or their waiting-maids throughout the church. Had they waited till the Dean had read the Collect,[1] it is possible that they might even then have changed their minds. It is curious at this distance of time to read as innocent and beautiful an expression of prayer as could be found in any part of the services of either Church:—

"Lord of all power and might, who art the Author of all good things, graft in our hearts the love of thy name, increase in us true religion, nourish us with all goodness, and of thy great mercy keep us in the same through Jesus Christ our Lord."

The other incident was apparently later in the day, when "a good Christian woman" who, unable to escape from the church after its doors were closed to quell the disturbance, had retired to the furthest corner to be beyond reach of the hateful service, and who then, hearing, as she thought, the "mass sang in her lug," turned round on the offender, and "shot against him the thunderbolt of her zeal, and warmed both his cheeks with the weight of her hands." The dreadful provocation which called for this explosion was, that "a young man sitting behind her began to sound forth 'Amen.'" [2]

Never, except in the days of the French Revolution, did a popular tumult lead to such important results. The stool which was on that occasion flung at the head of the Dean of Edinburgh extinguished the English Liturgy entirely in Scotland for the seventeenth century, to a great extent even till the nineteenth; and gave to the civil war of England

[1] Seventh Sunday after Trinity. [2] *Appendix to Lord Rothes*, p. 155.

an impulse which only ended in the overthrow of the Church and Monarchy.[1]

No doubt the exasperation had its root in the indomitable native vigor of which we have been speaking. But the intrinsic slightness of the incidents which roused it is the best proof of the force of the feeling. It is instructive as an instance of the folly of pressing outward forms, however innocent, on those who cannot understand them. It is an instructive reflection to both parties, that the main offenses which provoked this terrible manifestation might now be repeated with impunity in every Church in Scotland, Established, Free, or Seceding. It is an equally instructive reflection, that the two ecclesiastical communions that are now most closely allied against the existing constitution both of the Church of England and of the Church of Scotland, come from the spiritual descendants of Archbishop Laud in England, and the spiritual descendants of Jenny Geddes in Scotland.

The other scene to which I will call attention is the adoption of the National Covenant. Of all National Confessions of Faith ever adopted, at least in these realms, it is the one which for the

The National Covenant.

1 The whole transaction is ably described in Burton (vi. 442), who certainly shakes the identity of the "old herb-woman" with the Jenny Geddes who burnt her stool at the festivities of the Restoration.

The incidents, when read in the three original accounts of the *Large Declaration*, *Gordon's Scots' Affairs*, and the *Appendix to Lord Rothes' Memoirs*, are sufficiently distinct. It would seem that what particularly roused the first of the two assailants, was the inopportune correction of the Dean by the Archbishop, which called attention to the complication of the English service, when the Dean had to turn over the leaves to look for the Collect of the day; and that the second was excited by the sound of a *response* unusual in Presbyterian worship.

time awakened the widest and the deepest enthusiasm. It was in the Greyfriars' Church at Edinburgh that it was first received, on February 28, 1638. The aged Earl of Sutherland was the first to sign his name. Then the whole congregation followed. Then it was laid on the flat grave-stone still preserved in the church-yard. Men and women crowded to add their names. Some wept aloud, others wrote their names in their own blood; others added after their names "till death." For hours they signed, till every corner of the parchment was filled, and only room left for their initials, and the shades of night alone checked the continual flow. From Greyfriars' church-yard it spread to the whole of Scotland. Gentlemen and noblemen carried copies of it "in their portmanteaus and pockets," requiring and collecting subscriptions publicly and privately."[1] Women sat in church all day and all night, from Friday till Sunday, in order to receive the Communion with it. None dared to refuse their names. The general panic, or the general contagion, caught those whom we should least expect. The chivalrous Montrose, the gay Charles II., the holy and enlightened Leighton, were constrained to follow in the universal rush. From Scotland it spread to England; and there assumed the more portentous shape of the Solemn League and Covenant. What had begun by being an impassioned, yet not unreasonable, determination to defend the rights of Presbytery in Scotland, had now grown into a determination as impassioned to enforce it throughout the empire. The imperious dic-

The Solemn League and Covenant.

[1] Rothes, p. 46.

tation of the Church of Scotland reached into the heart of London. There, in St. Margaret's Church, beneath the shadow of Westminster Abbey, the Covenant was read from the pulpit, article by article, in the presence of both Houses of Parliament and of the Assembly of Divines. Every person in the congregation stood up, with his right hand raised to heaven, and took the pledge to observe it. One by one they signed their names; and thence it was spread and enforced with all the penalties of the law, and by all the pressure of enthusiasm, in every county in England. Hardly any ventured to decline. Forced explanations, mutual reservations, here and there were expressed. The voice of one just and wise man, Richard Baxter, was raised against this indiscriminate enforcement of so minute and terrible a confession. But, on the whole, it took its place as the very first and chiefest creed of the Church of Great Britain. The vehemence with which it was first received, the tenacity with which it still retains its hold on the Cameronian[1] portion of the Church of Scotland, is one of the most signal proofs of the power of Scottish religion to enkindle the whole nation. "I dinna ken what the Covenant is," said an old Scottish dame, even in our own day; "but I'll maintain it." "To pass in silence over the sworn Covenant" was, according to Rutherford,[2] a denial of Christianity itself. But, on the other hand, the rapid subsidence of this enthusiasm, even at the time; its almost total disappearance now even

[1] I have elsewhere given an instance of this from the practice of the Cameronians in Ulster. *Athanasian Creed*, p. 67.)

[2] *Letters*, p. 349. Bonar, p. 201.

amongst those who might be thought of the direct spiritual lineage of those who imposed it, is a striking example both to Scotland and all the world of the transitory nature of those outward expressions of party zeal, which at the moment seem all important. There are documents of a like sulphurous kind which still hold a certain place, though they were not engendered in so impassioned an atmosphere as the Solemn League and Covenant. But their original source is identical, and their ultimate fate will doubtless be the same.

Minute causes of division.

This leads me to the third point in Scottish theology which is worth noticing, namely, the littleness and the minuteness of the points on which its religious divisions have taken place. Perhaps in themselves they are not smaller or more obscure than some of those which divided the Church in the fourth and fifth centuries. But they have this peculiarity in Scotland, that they have hardly ever reached beyond the Scottish borders, or even the borders of the contending churches. The Solemn League and Covenant, as we have seen, for a few years had a vast extension through the whole realm. But the subsequent secessions, which have almost all had some relation to it, and which are in fact its direct offspring, are entirely confined to Scotland and Scottish colonies.

It is said that on the day of the Disruption of 1843, when the news flew through Edinburgh that four hundred ministers had left the Established Church, a well known judge exclaimed with a just feeling of national pride, "Have they gone out? There is not another country in the world in which such a spectacle could be seen." He was right. There was no other country in the world where so noble a testimony could have been borne to the sacredness and tenderness of scrupulous consciences. But it is no less true that, in no other country in the world would the consciences of so many able and excellent men have been so deeply wounded by the intricacies of a legal suit, of which the point at issue can only be ascertained by a searching investigation of conflicting statements, even amongst those who are most keen in the controversy. In the great Craigdallie case, which formed the analogous bone of contention between "the Old Lights and the New Lights," Lord Eldon expressed this difficulty with characteristic solemnity: "The Court,"[1] he said, "has pronounced an interlocutor, in which it describes the utter impossibility of seeing anything like what was intelligible in the proceedings, and I do not know how the House of Lords is to relieve the parties from the consequence. The Court of Session in Scotland are quite as likely to know what were the principles and standards of the Associate Presbytery and Synod of Scotland as any of your lordships; and are as well, if not better able, than your lordships, to decide whether any acts done or opinions professed by the defenders, Jedidiah Aiken and others, were opinions and facts which were a deviation on the part of the defenders from the principles and standards of the Associate Presbytery and Synod. If *they* were obliged to justify their finding as they do, intimating that they doubt whether they understood the subject at all, under the words, 'as far as they are capable of

[1] Innes's *Law of Creeds in Scotland*, pp. 341, 342.

understanding the subject,' I hope I may be permitted without offense to you to say, that there may be some doubt whether we understand the subject, not only because the Court of Session is much more likely to understand the matter than we are, but because I have had the mortification, many times over, to endeavor myself to understand what these principles were, and whether they have or have not deviated from them; and I have made the attempt to understand it, till I find it, at least on my part, to be quite hopeless."

The perplexity of Lord Eldon has often been felt by humbler inquirers. This extreme obscurity and particularity of theological statement of which he complains, has doubtless been the result of many causes. It belongs to the stubborn pugnacity of which I have just spoken. It belongs also to the extraordinary eagerness inherent in all movements of a party character, — but, from the union of logical subtlety and fervid impetuosity, particularly conspicuous in Scottish agitations, to invest small details with the grandeur of universal principles. There is a saying of Samuel Rutherford in his preface to the "Rights of Presbyterianism," which ought to be the exception in all sound theology, but which, in many of these Scottish disputes, has been taken as the rule. "In God's matters there is not, as in grammar, the positive and comparative degrees; there are not a true, and more true, and most true. Truth is in an indivisible line that hath no latitude."

This tendency may also have been in fact increased by the peculiarity of the Westminster Confession. Latest born, with one exception, of all

Protestant Confessions, it far more nearly approaches the full proportions of a theological practice, and exhibits far more depth of theological insight than any other. But, on the other hand, it reflects also far more than any other the minute hair-splitting and straw dividing distinctions which had reached their height in the Puritanical theology of that age, and which in sermons ran into the sixteenthly, seventeenthly sections, that so exercised the soul of Dugald Dalgetty as he waited for the conclusion of the discourse in the chapel of Inverary Castle. It accordingly furnished the food for which the somewhat hard and logical intellect of Scotland had a special appetite. The more genial influence of a general literature which had already sprung up in England, and which, as Matthew Arnold would say, had already played freely round its theological literature, and diffused something at least of "sweetness and light" into its darkest corners, had hardly yet made itself felt in Scotland. Questions of purely secular interest, patronage, decisions of courts of law, various details of civil administration, were thus invested with the dignity of fundamental principles, and pursued through all the ramifications of Covenanting theology.

Whitefield and the Seceders.

It would be ungracious, and it would be needless to multiply instances. Let one suffice. When George Whitefield came to Scotland, bursting with enthusiasm, burning with Calvinistic fervor, he expected nothing but sympathy from the disciples of John Knox, and especially from that extremest and straitest sect which, under the guidance of Ralph and Ebenezer Erskine, had, for the sake of purer air and more fiery zeal, deviated from the Church of Scotland as he had from the Church of England. "Come," said Ralph Erskine, with a simplicity which is almost tragical,—"come, if possible, dear Whitefield; there is no face on earth which I would more earnestly desire to see. Yet," he adds, "I do desire it only in a way that I think would tend most to the advancing of the Lord's kingdom, and Reformation-work *in our hands*." The humble mansion may still be visited at Dunfermline, in which Whitefield was received by the zealous brothers. A small low chamber, opening into a still smaller oratory, such as used till lately to be seen in many of the old houses in Edinburgh, was the scene of this singular conference. They required that he should only preach for them: they were the Lord's people. But Whitefield would hear of none of their limitations. He would refuse no call, he said, "to preach Christ, whoever gave it; were it a Jesuit or a Mohammedan, I would use it for testifying against them. If others are the devil's people, they have more need to be preached to. If the Pope should lend me his pulpit, I would declare the righteousness of Christ therein." They then determined to instruct him in the order of church government. He was required, before he proceeded a step further, to sign the Solemn League and Covenant. To their amazement he knew nothing about it, "as he had been busy with matters of greater importance." "Every pin of the tabernacle," they said, "was precious." He could not be persuaded, and they parted asunder.[1]

But they still pursued him and his work; and,

[1] Gledstone's *Life of Whitefield*.

after the wonderful effects produced by his preaching on the green bank at Cambuslang, still called "Conversion Brae," the Seceders, with the Cameronians at their back, appointed the 4th of August as a day of fasting and humiliation throughout their whole body, for the countenance given to Whitefield,[1] "a priest of the Church of England, who had sworn the Oath of Supremacy and abjured the Solemn League and Covenant, and for the system of delusion attending the present awful work on the bodies and spirits of men going on at Cambuslang." They published the "Declaration, Protestation, and Testimony of the suffering remnant of the anti-Popish, anti-Lutheran, anti-Erastian, anti-Prelatic, anti-Whitefieldian, anti-Sectarian, true Presbyterian Church of Christ in Scotland against George Whitefield and his encouragers, and against the work at Cambuslang and other places." In this protest the zealots and polemics of every Church may see their own faces reflected. Its spirit can hardly be said to have passed away from the Church of Scotland altogether. It would be most unjust and uncharitable to dwell on its manifestations as if they were general or predominant; and I shall, as I proceed, gladly acknowledge the immense advance made within the last thirty years, even in those quarters in which it chiefly prevailed. Yet surely it still is true, that hardly anywhere in Christendom could have been heard such animated and able debates as have been quite recently witnessed in the assembly of the greatest of the Seceding Churches in Scotland; one on "the Double and Single Reference," the other on "the Unlawfulness of Human Hymns."

[1] Burton lx. 201, 301.

II. It remains to sum up the good and evil of this aspect of Scottish theology, which has so deeply colored the Church of Scotland, which has been the one prevailing hue of those portions of it that make up the bulk of its outlying sections.

Fervid devotion.

1. On the one hand, it is undeniable that this has been the source at which some of the finest and noblest spirits of the Scottish Church, especially in its less educated classes, have been fed. The elaborate arguments of the Westminster Confession, and the long wail of the Judicial Testimony — the stubborn resistance to Popery and Prelacy — have formed the rough husk within which lies hid the Divine fire of Scotland's Burning Bush. If intolerant excesses of this tendency have given occasion to the withering sarcasms of Burns' "Holy Fair" and "Holy Willie," its nobler side has furnished that unrivaled picture of a poor man's religious household, — "The Cotter's Saturday Night": —

> "The cheerfu' supper done, wi' serious face,
> They, round the ingle, form a circle wide;
> The sire turns o'er, with patriarchal grace,
> The big ha' Bible, ance his father's pride:
> His bonnet rev'rently is laid aside,
> His lyart haffets wearing thin an' bare;
> Those strains that once did sweet in Zion glide,
> He wales a portion with judicious care,
> And 'Let us worship God!' he says, with solemn air."

Most true it is that "from scenes" and from studies like these "old Scotia's grandeur springs." The Solemn League and Covenant, strange as it seems to us, inspired a rapture seemingly as pure and heavenly as if it had been the "Imitatio Christi." Listen to the "Swan Song" — the very name is full of emotion — "or the dying testimony of that old, flourishing, and great Christian princely wrestler with his Master and valiant contender for Christ's truths and rights and royal prerogatives, James Masson." "When I first heard the Covenant mentioned, I thought my heart fluttered within me for joy. Then, therefore, at such times and in such places I took it, as at Dumfries, Pierpoint, Kirkmalo, and Iron Gray, which I never forget to this day, and hope never to do. O, what shall I speak to the commendation of those covenants? If they were then glorious and bright, I believe that they will be nine times as bright. And O, the sweet times of Covenanting I had likewise at communion in those days, when the Church was in her purity, and the Lord shined on W., and in other places, at the preaching of his word, which I cannot now tell over, being past my memory. But the back-looking to them now and then does not a little refresh my soul, as at Loche Hilt and Shallochburn, where, besides the sweet manifestations to my soul, and the soul of others then present, He was to be as a wall of fire round about us, defending us from our enemies." [1]

The splendid appeal of Ephraim Macbriar to his judges in "Old Mortality," which is almost literally copied from that of Hugh M'Cail, is as genuine an outcome of the wild theology of those days as the ravings of Habakkuk Mucklewrath. The tombs of the Covenanters are to the Scottish Church what the Catacombs are to the early Christian Church. If the inscriptions which hope that their persecutors will

"Find at Resurrection-day,
To murder saints was no sweet play," —

[1] Burton, viii. 253.

recall to us the savage imprecations of Tertullian, and the author of the treatise "De Mortibus Persecutorum," the simple ever-recurring rhymes which enumerate the names of those who died for the "covenanted work of Reformation," are more like the monuments of the Christians of those first ages than anything else which exists in modern times. In no other Protestant Church has such genuine veneration gathered round the graves of martyrs and scenes of martyrdom as at Auchinleck, where the whole parish migrated to the foot of the gallows on which Alexander Peden was hanged; or at Wigton, where the two women were drowned on the sea-shore for refusing the Test; or in the green spot called "the Martyrs' Field," on Magus Moor, through which no plough has ever been driven since the Covenanters were buried there who slew Archbishop Sharp. The outward circumstances which nourished this singular devotion have almost totally passed away. The devotion itself remains, a proof of the intensity of belief that can be sustained by the narrowest form of doctrine, if it be planted in a manly, independent understanding, and a warm, self-sacrificing heart.

"The soldiers of the Cameronian regiment," said Kerr of Kershaw, who, as Mr. Burton says, "being among them, but not of them," rendered to them this noble testimony, "are strictly religious, and make the war a part of their religion, and convert state policy into points of conscience. They fight as they pray, and pray as they fight. They may be slain; never conquered. Many have lost their lives; few or none ever yielded. Whenever their duty or their religion calls them to it, they are always unanimous and ready with undaunted spirit and great vivacity of mind to encounter hardships, attempt great enterprises, despise dangers, and bravely rush to death or victory."[1]

2. But, on the other hand, this marvelous energy of Scottish Presbyterian religion ought not to blind us to the fact of the curious defects by which the forms of it here considered have been so long disfigured. I do not now speak of the extravagances of Calvinism, which it shared with the Reformed Churches of Geneva, of Holland, and of Connecticut. But there are some features which it possesses almost peculiar to itself. The immense preponderance of the teaching of the Old Testament, and of some of the most transitory parts of the Old Testament over the New, and over the most essential part of the New, cannot but have cribbed, confined, and soured the religious teaching of the country. Even in Burns's beautiful picture of the "Cotter's Saturday Night," the scenes from Jewish history and from the most Judaic book in the "Christian volume" counterbalance all the rest. Much more was this the case in the earlier days, whence this form of teaching took its rise. The Scottish religious civil wars were, in the Acts of the General Assemblies, regarded as equivalent to the wars of the Lord in the Jewish times.[2] In a well known pamphlet of the seventeenth century — "Issachar's Ass braying under a Double Burden" — a careful observer has found that, out of a hundred or more references to the Bible, eighty-four are to the Old Testament and only fifteen to the New.[3] Of one of the most eminent lay politicians of the Covenanting Church, Lord Macaulay remarks,[4]

Judaic character of its theology.

1 Burton, vii. 460.

2 Cunningham, ii. 137.

3 Ibid. 256.

4 Macaulay, iii. 28.

that "He had a text of the Old Testament ready for every occasion. . . . It is a striking characteristic of the man, and of the school in which he had been trained, that in all the mass of his writing which has come down to us, there is not a word indicating that he had ever heard of the New Testament." The intense reverence for the Sabbath, beyond what is taught not only in the Roman Catholic or Anglican Churches, but in any Lutheran or Calvinistic Continental Church, is an example of the same tendency; a reverence, no doubt, which has fostered many of the finest qualities in the Scottish people, and which must be honored accordingly, but which assumed a disproportion, and became, so to speak, a malformation of the religious system analogous to that which is created in Russia by the excessive veneration for sacred pictures, and in France and Italy by the excessive veneration for particular saints.

Passing over some of the more obvious consequences of these peculiarities, there is one which deserves special notice, as probably the most direct result from the narrow, technical, and antagonistic basis on which Scottish religion has been constructed, and the numerous checks by which its free development is guarded. In one of Dr. Johnson's most insolent moods, when in the Isle of Skye, he attacked the ignorance of the Scottish clergy: "The clergy of England have produced the most valuable works in support of religion, both in theory and practice; what have your clergy done since they fell into Presbyterianism? Can you name one book of any value on a religious subject written by them?"[1] His oppo-

[1] Boswell, ii. 476.

nents were silent. The charge of general ignorance might, as we shall see hereafter, have been easily rebutted; and, as regards theology, if we pass from Dr. Johnson's time to our own, there are several living theologians of the Church of Scotland at whose feet Englishmen might be proud to sit. But the charge that no theological work had proceeded from Scotland which had more than a local reputation, is absolutely true with regard to the more strictly Presbyterian theology of which we are now speaking; and true, with a very few exceptions, which shall be noticed in their proper places, of Scottish theology altogether. A dearth so extraordinary in a nation whose struggles have been so profoundly religious, is a singular phenomenon. It may be in part explained, as Boswell tried to explain it, by the assiduity of the Scottish clergy in their parochial ministrations; in part by the poverty of the ecclesiastical endowments. But it must be chiefly explained by the technical and minute subjects on which Scottish theology has run. There are, doubtless, many treatises of Scottish theology — well known in Scotland — but the language, the matter, the thoughts are so restricted as to prevent them from ever reaching a wider circle of readers. "At the date," says Carlyle, "when Addison and Steele were writing their 'Spectators'" — (he might have added, when Jeremy Taylor and Barrow, when Locke and Cudworth were writing their treatises on theology and on Scripture, in works which are still reckoned amongst the glories of English literature) — "our good Thomas Boston was writing with the noblest intent, but in defiance of grammar and philosophy, his 'Four-

Absence of a general theology.

fold State of Man.' There were the schisms in our national Church, and the fiercer schisms in our body politic and theologic, ink, Jacobite blood, with gall enough in both to have blotted out the intellect of the country."[1] This general fact is a striking proof how strong a tendency there is in such angular religion, in these stringent obligations to a past system of theology, to dry up, as far as religion is concerned, the intellectual forces even of a highly intellectual people. It was under these straitening influences that the miserable superstitions of witchcraft lingered in Scotland after they had expired everywhere else; and that the strange delusions of what are called the "Men" long maintained a hold over the peasants and ministers of the Highlands.

Moral inconsistency.

And yet more. It is instructive to notice the instances, perhaps more striking from the sharpness of the contrast, in which the strong religious zeal of Scottish partisans has at times contrived to be united with worldly character or vicious life, such as we find in the history of some of the corresponding phenomena of the ecclesiastical history of France or of Russia. If any one imagines that Balfour of Burley in "Old Mortality" is an overdrawn caricature of this tendency, let them consider the undoubted historic instances of Lord Crawford and Lord Grange. Lord Crawford was appointed President of the Parliament by William III.'s government in the hope of conciliating the rigid Presbyterians. His exuberant use of the Old Testament has been already noticed. "Alone," says Lord Macaulay, " or almost alone of the eminent politicians,

[1] Carlyle, *Essays*, iii. 361.

he retained the religious style which had been fashionable in the preceding generation," and was by his own school confidently pronounced to be a saint.[1] "Yet," continues Lord Macaulay, "to those who judge of a man rather by his actions than his words, Crawford will appear to have been a selfish politician, who was not at all the dupe of his own cant, and whose zeal against Episcopal government was not a little whetted by his desire to obtain a grant of Episcopal domains."[2] Lord Grange was one of those grasping, vindictive, violent men that figure conspicuously in the earlier days of Scottish mediæval history. His wife, his kinsfolk, were the objects of his most cruel persecutions. "It is almost frightful," says Mr. Burton, "to find a man of this kind in firm alliance with the most rigid Presbyterian divines, conforming to the worship and discipline of their Church, so as to fulfill the most ample requisitions of the most exacting, and a powerful and well-trusted member of the Church courts. His diary of self-communing continues in a uniform strain the exalted tone of piety belonging to one who, as Wodrow says, thought there was too much preaching up of morality and too little of grace. Yet if there was any act of rigor, of indecent outrage on private life or opinion, Grange was the one to whom it was committed, and he performed the duty with genuine and unconcealed enjoyment."[3]

III. It may seem invidious thus to have dwelt on the darker traits of a great and noble people. If I have done so at more length than may have seemed becoming, it is because thus only could I draw out

1 Cunningham, ii. 445. 2 Macaulay, iii. 296. 3 Burton, viii. 309.

the peculiarities which are most instructive for them and for us to contemplate. In my two next lectures I shall hope to show that there has been in the Church, and may yet be, a more excellent way even than the Solemn League and Covenant, or the Judicial Testimony, or the fiery Baptism of the Disruption. But even in the aspect in which I have now been regarding the religion of Scotland, this excellent way may be discerned.

Religious excellence.

I have, in describing this fervid atmosphere, indicated how not only the Church of Scotland, in all its length and breadth, but the Church of England also may well warm its frozen heart, and get the chill out of its bones, by drawing near to the Burning Bush of Scotland's ancient Church. But that flame itself soars higher yet. It is at once a proof of the singular candor and the true religious instinct of Walter Scott, that of all the Scottish characters in his Scottish romances, none more truly represent the highest Christian type than Jeanie Deans, the daughter of an Anti-burgher, and Bessie Maclure, the mother of two martyrs for the Covenant.

Samuel Rutherford.

Let me dwell for a few moments on at least one historical character of this period, which doubtless may stand for many. I have already quoted a line from one of Milton's poems, in which he glances with contemptuous scorn at what he deemed the obscure name of Rutherford. He did not care to inquire what that name represented to the Scottish people. Samuel Rutherford is the true saint of the Covenant. His boyhood is enveloped with legends, such as those of which I spoke in my first lecture. His native place was Crailing, of which he himself afterwards said, "My soul's desire is that that place, to which I owe my first birth, in which I fear that Christ was scarcely named as touching any reality of the power of godliness, may blossom as the rose." It is said that the great-grandfather of the present Marquis of Lothian always raised his hat as he passed the cottage where Rutherford was born. A tradition ran that in his childish sports he had fallen into a well, and when his companions got back they found him on a hill, cold and dripping, but uninjured. "A bonnie white man," he said, "came and drew him out of the well." It is exactly the story of St. Cuthbert's childhood, repeated in the seventeenth century.[1]

His life.

Anwoth, on the shores of Galloway, was the scene of his pastoral ministrations. I have already spoken elsewhere of the traditions of his manse[2] and church, and described the scene of his interview with Archbishop Ussher. Men said of his life there, "He is *always* praying, *always* preaching, *always* entreating, *always* visiting the sick, *always* catechising, *always* writing and studying." "There," he says, "I wrestled with the angel, and prevailed. Woods, trees, meadows, and hills are my witnesses that I drew on a fair match betwixt Christ and Anwoth."[3]

We need not follow his life in detail. He was taken from Anwoth and imprisoned at Aberdeen, for his opposition to the policy of Charles I. He finally left Anwoth, after the triumph of the Covenant, to become Professor at St. Andrew's, where he remained till his end.

He was already on his death-bed when he was sum-

[1] *Life*, p. 6. [2] "The Eleventh Commandment." [3] *Life*, p. 186.

moned by the Parliament of Charles II. to appear before it on the charge of high treason. "I am summoned," he replied, "before a higher Judge and judicatory: that first summons I behove to answer; and, ere a few days arrive, I shall be where few kings and great folks come."

On the last day of his life, in the afternoon, he said, "This night will close the dawn and fasten my anchor within the veil, and I shall go away in a sleep by five o'clock in the evening. There is nothing now between me and the resurrection, but 'This day shalt thou be with me in paradise.' 'Glory, glory dwelleth in Emmanuel's Land.'"

When Parliament voted that he should not die in the College, Lord Burley rose and said, "Ye cannot vote him out of heaven." He lies in the churchyard of the ruined Cathedral of St. Andrew's; and, like a mediæval saint, has attracted round him "the godly, who desired that they might be laid even where his body was laid."[1]

I pass from his life to his character. An English merchant at St. Andrew's said: "I heard a sweet, majestic looking man [one of the other professors], and he showed me the majesty of God. Afterwards I heard a little fair man [Samuel Rutherford], and he showed me the loveliness of Christ." It is the same spirit as that in which, when Lord Kenmare once asked him, "What will Christ be like when He cometh?" he replied, "All lovely."[2]

His character.

The chief record of this is in his letters from "Christ's Palace at Aberdeen," as he termed his prison. They teem with figures of speech, so offen-

[1] Bonar's *Life*, p. 26. [2] *Life of Rutherford*, p. 107.

sive to the taste of a more refined age, that they are now, in great part, unreadable. Yet they were still, till the beginning of this century, a popular book of devotion in Scotland, England, and Holland. Richard Cecil, the most cultivated of modern English Evangelicals, said of him: "He is one of my classics, and he is a real original." Richard Baxter, the most latitudinarian of the fathers of Non-conformity, said, "Hold off the Bible, such a work the world never saw." And they contain passages which fully bear out this character: "With Samuel Rutherford,[1] the bitter and bigoted controversialist, let us have no fellowship. To Samuel Rutherford, the writer of those glowing letters, let the full sympathies of our soul be given."

Listen to his consolation to a lady on the death of a promising son. "I was once in your condition. I had but two children, and both are dead since I came hither. The supreme and absolute Father of all things giveth not an account of any of his matters. The good husbandman may pluck his roses, and gather in his lilies at midsummer, and, for aught I dare say, in the beginning of the first summer months; and he may transplant young trees out of the lower ground to the higher, where they may have the use of a purer air at any season of the year. What is that to you or to me? The goods are his own; the Creator of time and wind did a merciful injury (if I dare borrow the word) to nature, in landing the passenger so easily."[2]

1 "The Church and its Living Head;" a Sermon preached Nov. 13, 1859, by the Rev. J. Hanna, LL.D.

2 *Letters*, p. 308. Bonar, p. 136.

Listen to his description of the voyage of life: "How fast, how fast doth our ship sail! Ah! how fair a wind hath time to blow us off these coasts and this land of dying and perishing things! Ah, alas! our ship saileth one way, and fleeth many miles in one hour, to hasten us upon eternity, and our love and hearts are sailing close back over, and swimming towards ease, lawless pleasures, vain hopes, perishing riches, or to build a fool's nest I know not where, or to lay our eggs within the watermark, or fasten our bits of broken anchors on the worst ground in the world — this fleeting and perishing life; and, in the mean while, time and tide carry us on another life, and there is daily less and less oil in our lamp, and less and less sand in our watchglass. O, what a wise course it were for us to look away from the false beauty of our borrowed prison, and to mind and sigh for our country, 'Lord, Lord, take us home!'"

Listen to his lamentations for Scotland:[1] "Christ lieth like an old forecasten castle forsaken of its inhabitants; all men run away now from Him. Truth, innocent truth, goeth mourning, and wringing her hands in sackcloth and ashes. Woe, woe, woe to the virgin daughter of Scotland! woe, woe, woe to the inhabitants of this land! . . . . These things take me up so that a borrowed bed, another man's fireside, the wind upon my face (I being driven from my home and dear acquaintance, and my poor flock), find no room in my sorrow; I have no spare or odd sorrow for these; only I think the sparrows and swallows that build their nests in the kirk of Anwoth blessed birds."[2]

[1] *Letters*, p. 378. [2] Ibid. p. 363.

Listen to the expression of his better hope for his country: "I dare not speak one word against the all-seeing and ever-watching Providence of God. I see Providence runneth not on broken wheels; but I, like a fool, carried a provender for mine own ease, to die in my nest, and to sleep still till my gray hairs, and to lie on the sunny side of the mountain in my ministry at Anwoth. . . . . But now I see God hath the world on his wheels, and casteth it as a potter doth a vessel on the wheels!"[1] "O, that He would strike out windows and fair and great lights in this old house, this downfallen soul, that the rays and beams of light, and the soul-delighting glances of the fair, fair Godhead, might shine in at the windows and fill the house. A fairer and nearer and more direct sight of Christ would make room for his love, for we are pinched and straitened in his love. O, that he would break down the old narrow vessels of those narrow and shallow souls, and make fair, deep, wide, broad souls, to hold a sea and full tide, flowing over all its banks of Christ's love! . . . . O, what a heaven we should have on earth to see Scotland's moon like the light of the sun, and Scotland's sunlight manifold like the light of seven days, in the day that the Lord raiseth up the head of his people, and healeth the stroke of their wounds!"[2]

"We see God's working, and we sorrow. The end of his working still hidden, ... and therefore we believe not. Even amongst men we see hewn stones, timber, and a hundred scattered parcels and pieces of our house, all under tools, hammers, and axes, and saws. Yet the house — the beauty and care of so

[1] *Letters*, p. 378. [2] Ibid. p. 385.

many lodgings — we neither see nor understand for the present. These are not in the mind and head of the builder as yet. We see old earth, unbroken clods, graves, and stones; but we see not summer, lilies, roses, and the beauty of a garden."[1]

"Alas! that we will not pull and draw Him to his old tents again, to come and feed among the lilies till the day breaks and the shadows flee away. O, that the nobles would come, in the strength and courage of the Lord, to bring our lawful King Jesus here again. I am persuaded He shall return in glory to this land; but happy sure they who would help to convey Him to this country, and set Him up again on the mercy-seat between the cherubim. O Sun, return again to darkened Britain! . . . . I know He can also triumph in suffering, and weep, and reign, and die, and triumph, and remain in prison, and yet subdue his enemies. But how happy could I live to see the Coronation-day of Christ, to see his mother who bare Him put the crown upon his head again, and cry with shouting, till the earth shall sing, 'Lord Jesus, our King, live and reign for evermore.'"[2]

Conclusion.

That Coronation-day to Rutherford meant, no doubt, in its outward form, the enforcement of the Solemn League and Covenant, and almost every section of the Church of Scotland now existing would have seemed to him a miserable apostasy. But in the inner shrine of his devotions a higher spirit lingers, which we may humbly trust would find its solace even in our latter days. And so, in like manner, I would speak for a moment of

[1] *Letters*, 305. [2] Ibid. 350.

those who invest with the like sanctity modern watchwords and war-cries equally transitory. I have been told that in the "Convocation," or solemn assembly, that preceded the Disruption of 1843, a venerable minister exclaimed: "When I heard that the decisions of spiritual courts had been reversed by a decision of the House of Lords, I felt as an infant would feel if, whilst clinging to its mother's breast, it found that its mother had been suddenly shot dead." It was a pathetic appeal, which thrilled the whole Assembly. Yet if I might venture, from the experience of the past, to offer some consolation, I would suggest that the Church of Scotland has far too much life to be shot dead by any such external act as that to which the sacred orator referred. Again and again has that cry of the death of the Church of Scotland been raised: first, when the Covenant was broken; then when the Black Indulgence was granted; then when the Act of Union between England and Scotland was passed. On that last occasion was made the famous speech of Lord Belhaven, almost identical in words with those of the Free Church minister in 1843. All Scotsmen know it by heart: "I think I see our ancient mother Caledonia, like Cæsar, sitting in the midst of our senate, ruefully looking round about her, covering herself with her royal mantle, awaiting the fatal blow, and breathing out her last with the exclamation, 'And thou too, my son.'" The apprehension, the agitation, the very figure of speech of the illustrious statesman and the venerable ecclesiastic were the same, and sprang from the same source. And to both of them the same answer may be returned which was returned by Lord Marchmont to Lord Belhaven: "I awoke, and behold it was a dream." It was a dream to think that the great Scottish nation could be extinguished by incorporation with the civilization of England. It is a dream to think that the great Scottish Church was to be extinguished because it chose to submit to the decisions of law and the contact with the English State.

What forms of life Scottish religion still retains, and will retain if it be true to itself, I propose to consider in the next lectures.

LECTURE III.

THE MODERATION OF THE CHURCH OF SCOTLAND.

DELIVERED BEFORE THE PHILOSOPHICAL INSTITUTE,

JANUARY 11, 1872.

LECTURE III.

THE MODERATION OF THE CHURCH OF SCOTLAND.

Buckle's charge against the Church of Scotland.

IT will be remembered that Mr. Buckle, in his "History of Civilization," took Scotland as the example of the most bigoted, priest-ridden country in Europe, next to Spain; and drew a frightful picture of the Scottish clergy at the close of the seventeenth and the beginning of the eighteenth century.

The picture itself is probably overcharged; but, even if it were correct, the whole effect of the indictment is set aside by the fact — which Mr. Buckle has altogether overlooked — that in the period following this dark age, the Scottish clergy were the most liberal and enlightened of all the churches of Europe; nay, that even during the time that he imagines the Scottish Church to be lost in hopeless barbarism, there was a succession of men, who combined the deep religious sentiment which he admits, and the spirit of independence which he admires, with a just and philosophic moderation which, had he known, he could not have failed to admit and to admire equally.

The tendency which I am now about to describe is part of the prudential, "canny" side of the Caledonian character, and is as essential a feature of it as the *perfervidum*[1] *ingenium Scotorum*, which I ventured to depict in my last lecture. Let us trace it first in some of its earliest manifestations, and then in the Augustan age of its ascendency, where it found its home in the heart of the Established Church during what is called the reign of the Moderates.

Moderation in the age of the Reformation.

If the Church of Scotland had a Luther in Knox, it had an Erasmus in the wide and polished culture of George Buchanan;[2] and if his royal pupil had fulfilled the theological promise which he gave in his early years, Scotland might have had on her throne a monarch as latitudinarian as Maximilian II. of Germany, or as William the Silent of Orange. "He is neither Lutheran nor Calvinist," writes the Scottish correspondent to the French court, "but in many points much nearer to us. He thinks that faith is dead without works, that there is no predestination, and so forth. He holds a (false) opinion that Faith in God alone can save a man, let him belong to what religion he may."[3]

In the Regent Murray the fervor of the Reformation was combined with a forbearance strongly contrasted with the fierce temper of the age. "His house was compared to a holy temple, where no foul word was ever spoken. A chapter was read every day after dinner and supper in his family; yet no

1 It would seem that the original word in Buchanan (*Op.* i. 321) is *præfervidum*.

2 It has been said that George Buchanan, David Hume, and Walter Scott are the three Scottish writers of European influence and celebrity. See a very interesting article on Buchanan in the *North British Review*, No. xci. March, 1867.

3 Froude, xi. 665.

one was more free from sour austerity, and he had quarreled once with Knox, 'so that they spoke not together for eighteen months,' because his nature shrank from extremity of intolerance, because he insisted that his sister should not be interdicted from mass."[1] With true Scottish humor and sagacity he took up his post at the door, and declared with much solemnity that he had placed himself there "that no Scotsman might pollute his eyes with the abominable thing."[2]

John Knox himself had a tinge of moderation which has been but little recognized either by his friends or his enemies. His Confession of Faith stands alone amongst Protestant Confessions for the acknowledgment, far in advance of its age, of its own fallibility: "We protest that if any one will note in this our Confession any article or sentence impugning God's Holy Word, that it would please him of his goodness, and for Christian charity's sake, to admonish us of the same in writing; and we, upon our honor and fidelity, do promise unto him satisfaction from the mouth of God (that is, from his Holy Scriptures), or else reformation of that which he shall prove to be amiss."[3] The rigid Sabbatarianism of modern times received no sanction either from his practice or his teaching. He supped with Randolph on one Sunday evening, and visited Calvin during a game of bowls on another.[4] The austere theology of Andrew Melville was tempered

1 Froude, xi. 502.

2 Cunningham, i. 376.

3 This is admirably brought out by Dr. Robert Lee in his Address on the Position of the Clergy.

4 Hessey's *Bampton Lectures*, v. 269, 270.

by an interest in classical and academical literature, the very reverse of a hard[1] and narrow Puritanism.

As in England, so in Scotland, there were gentle or prudent spirits who, in spite of the wide chasm between the ancient and the Reformed Church, still in a measure belonged to both. Such was Hugh Rose, the Black Baron of Kilravoch. "He lived in a very divided, factious time; there falling out then great revolutions in Church and State, religion changed from Popery to Protestant — the Queen, laid aside, being in exile. Yet such was his ever ingenuous, prudential carriage, that he wanted not respect from the most eminent of all the parties." What was said of a debate betwixt him and two neighbors might be said of his whole life. "Hutcheon Rose, of Kilravoch, an honest man, ill guided betwixt them both."[2] Such, perhaps in a less creditable form, was John Winram, sub-prior of St. Andrew's, who through the whole of that troubled period retained his office, and has the fact recorded on his tombstone in St. Leonard's church-yard. *Conversis Rebus,* — "though the world had even turned upside down," he contrived still to live and die sub-prior of St. Andrew's.

Early Erastianism.

Again, the Erastian element in the Scottish Church — its close connection with the State, and with all the influences of the State, was exceedingly strong from its very first beginning. The original Confession of John Knox[3] contains nothing

[1] See the interesting account of his scheme for the university of St. Andrew's. M'Crie, *Life of Melville*, ii. 358.

[2] Cosmo Innes's *Early Scottish History*, p. 440. See also his summary of the whole family.

[3] Innes, *Law of Creeds*, p. 23. Knox's *History*, pp. 208–216. See also his *Appellation to the Nobility and Estates of Scotland*, in 1556.

on the independence of the Church; and it, as well as the Westminster Confession, afterwards was made binding on the Scottish Church by Act of Parliament.[1]

The General Assembly, as I have already said, was itself a kind of parliament. Its forms were borrowed not from the Councils of the Church, but from the Scottish Parliaments. The *ouvertures* of the Parliament are the *overtures* of the Assembly.[2] It was a very different body then from that to which, by successive purifications of the lay element, it has since been reduced. The King, the Regent, the Privy Councillors, the Barons, had a seat and a vote in it when they chose to exercise them. The qualification of King as elder was not insisted on. When the great laymen came in any numbers the ministers were compelled to sit outside the bar. The presence of the Regent and the nobility was felt by the Assembly itself to be "most comfortable and most earnestly wished of all, and his absence most dolorous and lamentable."[3]

In the Westminster Assembly the advance of Scottish theology depended considerably on the advance[4] of the Scottish army. The English members of parliament were always passing in and out of the Jerusalem Chamber, and kept a constant watch over its deliberations.

1 The original movement of the Scottish Reformation was not so much popular as baronial. The great lords held the cause in their own hands, and by their influence mainly it was decided.

2 Burton, i. 567.

3 See Turner's *History of the Secession*, c. v. Cunningham, i. 481, 483.

4 Read Baillie's *Letters*. "He allows that the pressure of the Scottish army helped forward the acceptance of the Scottish theology in Westminster." Chalmers' *Life*, iii. 437.

The Covenant, as we have seen, invoked in the strongest terms the aid of the State, and only turned against the State when the State turned against the Covenant.

This brings us from the fierce struggles of the fifteenth to those of the seventeenth century. Even on the face of the general movement there are traces of a milder spirit.

The Westminster Confession, complete as it seemed to be, was yet from the first seen to partake of the latitude and largeness of a compromise. It contained no special mention of divine order, or necessity of the ecclesiastical offices recognized in the Presbyterian Church. In the regulations for the Eucharist[1] there is nothing to guard against a free communion. Professor Mitchell, of St. Andrew's, has ably pointed out the liberal tendency of many of its statements, as might be expected from an assembly which contained such men as Selden, Lightfoot, and Calamy. Still more clearly is this visible in individual examples.

It has been sometimes complained that Walter Scott's character of Henry Morton in "Old Mortality," with his enlarged views and philosophic Christianity, is an anachronism. But to any student of those times it is evident that the great master was in this instance as faithful to historical truth as when he painted Mause Headrigg or Sergeant Bothwell. Not only is the prototype of Morton to be found in

[1] Confession, xxvi. 21. The special precautions which limited this freedom as well as the more stringent forms of subscription, were the work of later ecclesiastical legislation, and were intensified in the seceding Churches. See Grub, iii. 125, and Moncrieff's *Life of Erskine*, p. 139.

the contemporary school of the English Latitudinarians who had gathered round Lord Falkland in the vale of Great Tew, or round Cudworth in the Platonic repose of Cambridge; but in Scotland also his likeness may again and again be traced. Just such a man — half Presbyterian and half Episcopalian — had been Patrick Forbes, the laird of Corse, who in early youth had been the friend of Andrew Melville, and who in later life reluctantly accepted the bishopric of Aberdeen from James I. "If wherein our doubt seemeth defection, his Highness would so far pity our weakness and consider our peace as to enforce nothing but what first in a free and national council were determined, wherein his Highness would neither make any man afraid with terror, nor pervert the judgment of any with hope of favor, then men may adventure to do service. But if things be so violently carried as no end may appear of bitter contention, nor any place left to men in office but to stir the coals of detestable debate, for me I have no courage to be a partner in that work. I wish my heart's blood might extinguish the ungracious rising flame in our Church."[1] That is Henry Morton all over. That is the true statesmanlike and Christianlike policy which might yet have saved Episcopacy and Presbyterianism alike from their worst excesses. And Patrick Forbes was no hireling priest or skeptical philosopher. He had become a lay preacher at the urgent entreaty both of his Episcopalian and Presbyterian neighbors; and he became a bishop in the hope of moderating the passions of the Episcopal party. If even he, too, was afterwards led away by the frenzy

[1] See Bishop Forbes's *Funerals*. Grub, ii. 34.

of the time, yet he retained enough of his original goodness to call down the eulogy, not only of those whom he joined, but even of some of those whom he had left. Wodrow regarded him as the "best of the Scottish prelates;" and the Aberdeen colleges remained a monument of his enlightened zeal, when almost every trace of the Scottish Episcopate perished.

But it is in the history of the next generation that this element of Scottish religion began to exercise a wider influence.

Look at the deputation of Scottish ministers who went up to London for the rearrangement of the Church at the time of the Restoration. Some of them were obscure enough; but two were men of sufficient interest to redeem the character of any school of thought from insignificance or contempt. One was Robert Douglas. He held the highest place in the Scottish Church. He had been twice moderator. He had preached the coronation sermon of Charles II. at Scone. He was one of the chief promoters of the Restoration. He was a stanch Presbyterian, convinced of the divine right of Presbytery, full of zeal for the Covenant.[1] But he was always against extreme measures. "He was," says Burnet, who knew him in his old age, "a reserved man — too calm and grave for the furious men, yet much depended on for his prudence" — too prudent, indeed, Burnet thought him — "for he durst not own the free thoughts he had of some things for fear of offending the people." His theology was thus described by the partisans who were eager to scent out those free

Robert Douglas.

[1] Wodrow, ii. 329.

thoughts: "*He had a singular way of preaching, without doctrines, which some called scumming the text.*"[1] He regarded Ruthford's fanatical "Protestation" in behalf of the Covenant as "the highest breach of all the articles of the Covenant that ever was since the work of Reformation began." He was "a great State preacher, one of the greatest of that age in Scotland — for he feared no man to declare the mind of God to him — yet very accessible, and easy to be conversed with. Unless a man were for God, he had no value for him, let him be never so great and noble."[2]

He lived on gracious terms with his opponents. Of one of the ministers with whom he had variance on some ecclesiastical matters, he said, "I love him *as* my own soul." Against Sharpe, no doubt, he spoke angrily, but probably because he believed him insincere. "Take it, James," he said, when there was the question of the archbishopric of St. Andrew's; "take it, and the curse of God be on you for your treacherous dealing."[3] "Brother, no more brother, James. If my conscience had been as yours," he said to Sharpe, "I could have been Bishop of St. Andrew's before you." "But," he added to some one else, "I will never be Archbishop of St. Andrew's unless I be Chancellor of Scotland also, as some were before me." He was, in fact, a statesman as much as a divine. He had served as chaplain in the army of Gustavus Adolphus; and that great king was reported to have said of him when he took leave: "There is a man who, for wisdom and prudence,

1 Wodrow's *Analecta*, i. 166; iii. 82, 83, 298.

2 Wodrow's *Analecta*, iii. 82, 83.

3 Burton, vii. 405. Scott's *History of Scotland.*

might be counselor to any prince in Europe; he might be a moderator to a General Council; and even for military skill I could very freely trust my army to his conduct." Yet in his statesmanship he never lost his sacred character. He had, whilst in the army of Gustavus, got the most part of all the Bible in his memory, having then taken no other book to read, so that "he was as a concordance to the exactness of a Jew."[1]

He was one of those whom we sometimes meet in history, evidently far greater than circumstances permitted them to show themselves. There was a majesty and authority in his face that caused those who looked at him to stand in awe of him; "an air of greatness," says Burnet, "that made all that knew him inclined to believe he was of no ordinary descent." If anything could enhance the interest of this mysterious, lofty-minded man, — "the great Mr. Douglas," as he was called, — it would be the extraordinary parentage to which these words of Burnet point. True or false, the romantic story was cherished in the popular belief that his grandfather was George Douglas of Lochleven, and his grandmother the illustrious captive of that famous castle.[2]

If of Douglas we unfortunately know but little, we are fully informed as to one of his companions. Robert Leighton was the one saint common both to the Presbyterian and the Episcopalian Church. His whole education and early ministry was Presbyterian. His outward form of doctrine was a temperate Cal-

[1] Burnet, *Own Time*, i. 34. Wodrow's *Analecta*, iii. 82.

[2] Burnet, i. 34. Wodrow's *Analecta*, i. 166. Burton, v. 103; vii. 405, 406.

vinism. The work by which he is chiefly known, his "Commentary on St. Peter's Epistles," was written when he was in charge of the parish of Newbattle. It was only in later life that, for a few years, he reluctantly entered, and then gladly quitted the office of Bishop and Archbishop, which he had chiefly used for the sake of reconciling Presbyterianism and Episcopacy together.

Robert Leighton.

He was, indeed, a man whom either church might be glad to claim. But the peculiarity of his position was, that he combined a sanctity equal to that of the strictest Covenanter or the strictest Episcopalian, with a liberality in his innermost thoughts equal to that of the widest Latitudinarian of the school of Jeremy Taylor or of Hoadley. Let us look at both these points more minutely. They both appear far more strongly in the records of his life and conversation than could be inferred from his published writings.

There are few men whose character gives the impression of a more complete elevation both above the cares and the prejudice of the world — of a more entire detachment from earth.

His devotion.

Sometimes this appeared in his playful sayings on the misfortunes of life. On some great pecuniary loss he made a jesting remark. "What!" said his relation; "is that all you make of the matter?" "Truly," answered Leighton, "if the Duke of Newcastle, after losing nineteen times as much of yearly income, can dance and sing, while the solid hopes of Christians will not avail to support us, we had better be as the world." Once as a party embarked on the Thames in a boat between the Savoy and Lambeth, the boat was in imminent danger of sinking, and most of them crying out, Leighton never lost his serenity; and, to some who expressed their astonishment, replied, "Why, what harm would it have been if we had all been safe landed on the other side!"

More often he expressed this gravely. "It is in vain," he would say, "for any one to speak of divine things, without something of divine affections. An ungodly clergyman must feel uneasy when preaching godliness, and will hardly preach it persuasively. He has not been able to prevail on himself to be holy, and no marvel if he fail of prevailing on others. In truth he is in danger of becoming hardened against religion by the frequent inculcation of it, if it fail of melting him."

He felt deeply the weariness of the world and of the Church. "I have met with many cunning plotters, but with few truly honest and skillful undertakers. Many have I seen who were wise and great as to this world; but of such as are willing to be weak that others may be strong, and whose only aim it is to promote the prosperity of Zion, I have not found one in ten thousand."

To the Lord's Prayer he was specially partial, and said: "O! the spirit of this prayer would make rare Christians."[1] "One devout thought is worth all my books."[2] The Psalter he called "a bundle of myrrh that ought to lie day and night in the bosom."[3] Scarce a line in it that had passed without the stroke of his pencil. "My uncle did not give thanks," observed his little nephew, "like other folks."[4] His

1 Pearson's *Life of Leighton*, vol. i. p. cxiii.

2 Ibid. p. cxiv.

3 Ibid. p. cxvi.

4 Ibid. p. cxviii.

longing to depart grew into a passion. "To be content to stay always in this world," he said, "is above the obedience of angels. Those holy spirits are employed according to the perfection of their natures, and restlessness in hymns of praise is their only rest. But the utmost we poor mortals can attain to is to lie awake in the dark, and a great piece of art and patience it is *spatiosam fallere noctem*." Often would he bewail the proneness of Christians to stop short of perfection; and it was his grief to observe, that "some good men are content to be *low and stunted vines*."[1]

This is a letter to a friend when he was Principal of the University of Edinburgh: "O! what a weariness is it to live amongst men and find so few men, and amongst Christians and find so few Christians; so much talk and so little action; religion turned almost into a tune and air of words; and, amidst all our pretty discourses, pusillanimous and base, and so easily dragged into the mire; self and flesh, and pride and passion domineering, while we speak of being in Christ and clothed with Him, and believe it, because we speak it so often and so confidently.[2] Well, I know you are not willing to be thus gulled, and, having some glances of the beauty of holiness, aim no lower than perfection, which is the end we hope to attain, and in the mean time the smallest advances towards it are more worth than crowns and sceptres. I believe it you often think on those words of the blessed Apostle Paul [on the corruptible and incorruptible reward]. There is a noble guest within us. O let all our business be to entertain Him honorably,

1 Pearson's *Life of Leighton*, vol. i. p. cxix. 2 Ibid. p. ciii.

and to live in celestial love within; that will make all things without to be very contemptible in our eyes. I should run on did I not stop myself. Therefore, 'good night' is all I add, for whatever hour it comes to your lot, I believe you are as sensible as I that it still is night; but the comfort is, it draws nigh towards that bright morning."

This eagerness resulted from his earnest desire "to see and enjoy perfection in the perfect sense of it, which he could not do and live. That consummation is a hope deferred, but when it cometh it will be a tree of life." He longed to escape from the public toils in which he was involved, "if only into the air, among the birds." "Though I have great retirement here at Dunblane," he writes to his sister,—"as great and possibly greater than I could find anywhere else,—yet I am still panting for a retreat from this place, and all public charge, and next to rest in the grave. It is the pressingest desire of anything I have in this world; and, if it might be, with you or near you." To close his life was, he said, "like a traveller pulling off his miry boots." His well-known wish was to die in an inn—"the whole world being a large and noisy inn, and he a wayfarer tarrying in it as short a time as possible." So, in fact, he breathed his last in the Bell Inn, Warwick Lane.

His latitudinarianism.

With this singular spirit of devotion was combined a freedom of thought and elevation above the common prejudices of saints, which give him a rare place amongst divines. He was fully aware of the difficulties which beset the popular problems of theology. To his nephew, who complained that there was a certain text of Scripture which he could not understand, his answer was, "And many more that I cannot." Being once asked about the saints reigning with Christ, he eluded the question by replying, "*If* we suffer with Him, we shall also reign with Him;" and, when pressed still further, answered at last: "If God hath appointed any such thing for us He will give us heads to bear such liquor. Our preferment will not make us reel." To curiosity on such points he answered in the words of the angel to Manoah, "Why askest thou thus after my name, seeing it is secret?" "Enough," he said, "is discovered to satisfy us that righteousness and judgment are within, though round about his throne are clouds and darkness." "That prospect of predestination and election," he said, "is a great abyss into which I choose to sink rather than attempt to sound it. And truly any attempt to throw light upon it makes it only a greater abyss."

He fully entered into the doubts and difficulties of others; and, even whilst most condemning them, believed them to be quite compatible with a true love of God. "Whatever be the particular thoughts or temptations that disquiet you, look above them and below to fix your eyes on that infinite goodness which never faileth them that (by naked faith) do absolutely rely and rest upon it, and patiently wait on Him who hath pronounced them all (without exception) blessed that do so." "Say often within your own heart, 'Though He slay me yet will I trust in Him.' And if, after some intervals, your troubled thoughts do return, check them still with the holy Psalmist's words, 'Why art thou so cast down, O my soul?'"

Whilst disposed almost to a monastic seclusion of

religious meditation, — to the practice, as he would say, of constantly dressing and undressing his soul in devotional exercises, — he yet felt that a mixed life was the most excellent.[1] He ventured to call it, thus reversing the common use of the word, "an angelical life;" as being "a life spent between ascending to fetch blessings from above and descending to scatter them among mortals." He hated the notion of "dressing religion with a hood and bells."[2]

He was the only man of that age — we may almost say of any age — that deliberately set himself, as to the work of his life, to the union of the two Churches. He was absolutely indifferent to the forms of either. "The mode of church government," he said "is unconstrained; but peace and concord, kindness and good will are indispensable. But, alas! I rarely find men bound with a holy resolution to contend for the substance more than the ceremony, and disposed in weak and indifferent things to be weak and compliant."[3]

It was this supreme indifference to forms, and this intense desire of union which caused him not only to accept, however unwillingly, the office of a bishop, but to accept the conditions of being reordained by Episcopal ordination. It was nothing to him how often he was reordained. It was in his eyes a mere form which conveyed of itself no additional sanctity; and, therefore, whilst the worldly Sharpe hesitated, the holy Leighton saw no difficulty. It was the like indifference, which, when he came to Scotland, induced him to use every means of conciliation to enable Presbyterians to come into friendly terms with

1 Pearson, p. cxiv. 2 Ibid. p. cxvi. 3 Ibid. p. cxiii.

the bishops. He entreated the Episcopalians to abstain from imitating the severities of the Covenanters, justifying the sarcasm, that "the world goes mad by turns."[1]

Strictly Protestant as he was, whether as taken from his dogmatical or his latitudinarian side, he yet had an indulgence even for Roman Catholics, at that time very unusual. To a "highflying Scotsman," who said to him, "Sir, I hear your grandfather was a Papist, your father a Presbyterian, and you a bishop — what a mixture is this!" he replied, "It 's true, sir; and my grandfather was the honestest man of the three."[2] Some one was told to ask him what he thought of the Beast, adding, "I told the inquirer that you would certainly answer you could not tell." "Truly you said well," replied Leighton; "but if I was to fancy what it were, it would be something with a pair of horns that pusheth his neighbors, as both have so much practiced of late in Church and State." He strongly condemned the zeal of proselytizers, whether Roman or Protestant, "who fetched ladders from hell to scale heaven." "I prefer," he said, "an erroneous honest man to the most orthodox knave in the world; and I would rather convince a man that he has a soul to save, and induce him to live up to that belief, than bring him over to any opinions in whatsoever else beside. Would to God men were but as holy as they might be in the worst of forms now among us. Let us press them to be holy, and miscarry if they can." Being told of a person who had changed his persuasion, all he said was, "Is he

[1] Pearson, p. cxiii.

[2] Wodrow's *Analecta*, i. 26.

more meek — more dead to the world? If so, he has made a happy change."[1]

His aphorisms are full of spiritual wisdom. "One half the world lives upon the weakness of the other." "All things operate according to the disposition of the subject." "It is better to send a congregation home still hungry than surfeited." "*Deliver me, O Lord,*" he used to say, "*from the errors of wise men, yea and of good men.*"[2]

One single expression, perhaps, best shows the secret at once of his unworldliness, his humor, and his high philosophy. He was reprimanded in a synod for not "preaching up the times." "Who," he asked, "does preach up the times?" It was answered that all the brethren did it. "Then," he rejoined, "if all of you preach up the times, you may surely allow one poor brother to preach up Christ Jesus and Eternity!"[3]

Such a breadth of view provoked, as was to be expected, the suspicions and attacks of narrow zealots. "Mr. Guthrie used to say, in the time of hearing him preach he was as in heaven; but he could not bring one word with him almost out of church doors — referring to his haranguing way of preaching without heads."[4]

He was thought to be "lax in his principles anent the divinity of Christ, and upon the matter an Arian"[5] — "very much suspected to be an Arian, and vented several things that way." Mr. David Dickson complained of his expositions on charity.

1 Pearson's *Life of Leighton*, vol. i. p. cxxvii.

2 Ibid. p. cxvi.

3 Ibid. vol. i. p. xvi.

4 Wodrow's *Analecta*, ii. 348.

5 Ibid. i. 274; ii. 212.

"People should not make a fool of their charity." Leighton replied, "I do not know what you mean, but the Scripture makes a fool of charity, for it says, 'Fools bear all things, and charity beareth all things.'" The austere Wodrow cannot forbear to add the comment on this playful remark, — "A very light expression."[1]

He gave great scandal at Edinburgh by recommending "Thomas à Kempis" as one of the best books ever written, next to the inspired writers. "Mr. Dickson refused it, because, amongst other reasons," he added, "neither Christ's satisfaction nor the doctrine of grace, but self and merits run through it."[2]

What the effect of Leighton's character was on his contemporaries appears from the remarks of Burnet. Totally unlike as that forward, restless, active prelate must have been to the retiring and sensitive Leighton, his testimony is the more striking. "I bear still the greatest veneration for the memory of that man that I do for any person, and reckon my early knowledge of him, and very long and intimate connection with him for twenty-three years, among the greatest blessings of my life, and for which I know I must give account to God in the great day in a most particular manner. He had the greatest elevation of soul, the largest compass of knowledge, the most sanctified and heavenly disposition that I ever yet saw in mortal. He had the greatest parts as well as virtues with the perfectest humility that ever I saw in man. He had a sublime strain in preaching with so grave a gesture, and such a majesty both of

1 Wodrow, *Analecta*, iii. 452. 2 Ibid. ii. 349.

thought, of language, and of pronunciation, that I never once saw a wandering eye when he preached, and have seen whole assemblies often melt in tears before him. I never heard him say an idle word that had not a direct tendency to edification, and I never once saw him in any temper but that which I wished to be in at the last moments of my life."

Memorials of Leighton.

We can still figure to ourselves the Cathedral of Dunblane, as it appeared during his ministrations. The beautiful nave was probably as it is now — complete in all its proportions, save the roof. The choir was lined with the old stalls of the fifteenth century; but round the walls ran an unsightly gallery now removed. The Bishop's house opened on the grassy slopes leading down to the Allan, along whose steep banks was an avenue of trees, still known by the name of the Bishop's Walk; and the library founded by him yet remains, alone of inhabited ecclesiastical edifices in Scotland retaining a mitre over the door.

In England, his burial-place at Horsted Keynes is still venerated, and his "Commentary on St. Peter," alone of ancient Scottish works of theology, is read on the south of the Tweed; and the "Aphorisms" drawn from it have been made the basis of one of the most philosophical of English theological treatises, — Coleridge's "Aids to Reflection."

It is not without reason that I have dwelt at such length on the character of Leighton. Not only does such a character of itself consecrate the Church in which he was born and bred, but it sheds its own lustre on the special tendency which it exemplified. However much, in later days, the Moderate party in the Church of Scotland may have seemed to become "of the earth earthy," it is something for them to be able to claim, as their pattern, the most apostolical of all Protestant Scotsmen. However chimerical may seem in our days an equal respect to Episcopacy and Presbyterianism, it is enough that the projected—the all but completed—union between them originated in a head so clear and a heart so pure as Leighton's.

Charteris.

We pass on to another, who is also commemorated by Burnet, Lawrence Charteris, minister of the beautiful village of Dirleton, who was "often moved to accept a bishopric, but always refused it." "He was a perfect friend and a most sublime Christian. He did not talk of the defects of his time like an angry reformer, that set up in that strain because he was neglected or provoked; but like a man full of a deep but humble sense of them. He was a great enemy to large confessions of faith, chiefly when they were imposed in the lump, as tests; for he was positive in few things. He had gone through the chief parts of learning; but was most conversant in history as the innocentest sort of study, that did not fill the mind with subtlety, but helped to make a man wiser and better."[1] It is impossible to imagine anything breathing more fully the best spirit of Christian latitude than his address to his people on the Fast Day of 1690: "All who are wise and who have a right sense of true religion and Christianity, cannot but see there has been a great defection among us. The defection has not been from the truth, or from the funda-

[1] Burnet, *Own Time*, i. 216.

mental articles of the Christian faith, but from the life of God and the power of religion, and from the temper and conversation which the Gospel requires of us."[1]

The word "Moderation."

We have arrived at the momentous period when the Church of Scotland entered on the outward conditions of existence under which it has continued ever since. It was now that there began the full ascendency of that great philosophic virtue and Evangelical grace in the Church of Scotland, of which the name has in these latter days been used as though it were the title of a deadly heresy, but which the Apostle has employed to designate one of the most indispensable of Christian duties in the impressive precept, "Let your moderation[2] be known unto all men." What the Apostle thus enjoined was the key-note of the address of the King's Commissioner, Lord Carmichael, when after an interval of forty years the General Assembly resumed its functions in 1690: "We expect that your management shall be such as we shall have no reason to repent of what we have done. A calm and peaceable procedure will be no less pleasing to us than it becometh you. We never could be of the mind that violence was suited to the advancing of true religion; nor do we intend that our authority shall ever be a tool to the irregular passions of any party. MODERATION is what religion requires, neighboring churches expect from, and we recommend to you."

[1] The whole address is given in Grub, ii. 327.

[2] The original word, no doubt, has that deeper meaning which an accomplished critic has rendered "sweet reasonableness." Still, the word "moderation," for any single phrase, is probably the best that could be found.

This was the true "Revolution settlement," in the highest sense of the word — this was the call to which, on the whole, the Church of Scotland from that time since has remained faithful.

Revolution settlement.

The first great preacher of this new national Covenant, — the oracle which, we can hardly doubt, inspired that royal recommendation to the General Assembly, was one of the most illustrious benefactors of the Scottish Church and nation.[1] It was the singular fortune of King William III. to have had for his two most intimate advisers and friends, two of the most eminent ecclesiastics of Great Britain, both of them Scots. In the south, next to the Primate Tillotson, was Gilbert Burnet, Bishop of Salisbury. In the north the real Presbyterian Primate of the Church of Scotland, William Carstairs.

Carstairs.

Carstairs has left nothing in writing; but his life is filled full of Christian strength and wisdom. His earliest public appearance was undergoing the agonizing trial of the thumbscrew before the Privy Council in Edinburgh. All present, even his judges, were struck by the extraordinary fortitude and generosity of a man "who stood more in awe of his love for his friends than of the fear of torture, and hazarded rather to die for them than that they should die for him."

Recommended to the Prince of Orange by this

[1] The anecdotes here given are mostly taken from M'Cormick's Preface to Carstairs' State Papers. Since delivering this lecture I have been delighted to hear that the task of publishing a complete memoir of Carstairs has fallen into worthy hands, — the Rev. Herbert Story, of Rosneath, who, as a descendant of the sister of that eminent man, has been intrusted with the original letters.

heroic courage, as well as by the singular sagacity which he showed on the same occasion in revealing to his judges only what was of no use to them and no harm to any one else, he accompanied William on his eventful voyage to England, and was the first, Scotsman and Presbyterian as he was, to call down the blessings of Heaven on the expedition, by the religious service which he celebrated immediately on his landing at Torbay, after which the troops all along the beach, at his instance, joined in the 118th Psalm. From that time he was William's companion to every field of battle — his most trusty adviser in all that related to the affairs of Scotland. "Cardinal Carstairs" was the name by which he was usually known, alluding to the saying of Cardinal Ximenes that he could play at football with the heads of the Castilian grandees. The King had one all-sufficing explanation of his influence: "I have known Mr. Carstairs long; I have known him well; and I know him to be an honest man." One famous instance of his power is recorded, unique in the history of princes and churches. An oath ("the oath of assurance," as it was called), extremely obnoxious to the General Assembly, had been intended by the English Government to be imposed on its members. The Commissioner sent up an earnest remonstrance against it by a special messenger. There was just time for him to return to Scotland with the King's final determination on the night before the Assembly was appointed to meet. Carstairs was absent when the messenger arrived; and in that interval William, under the advice of his ministers, refused to listen to the remonstrance, and sent off his instructions by the messenger. When Carstairs arrived at Kensington, he heard what had happened. He found the messenger setting off for Scotland, and demanded him in the King's name to deliver up the dispatches. It was now late at night; not a moment was to be lost. He ran to the royal apartment, and was told by the lord in waiting that the King was in bed. He insisted on entering and found William fast asleep, drew the curtain, threw himself on his knees by the bedside, and awakened him. The King, startled, asked what had brought him, and for what he knelt. "I am come to ask my life." "What can you have done," said William, "to deserve death?" Carstairs told what had occurred. The King was furious; Carstairs begged only for a few words to explain. The King listened, was convinced, threw the dispatch into the fire, wrote a new one at the dictation of Carstairs; the messenger set off, and, in consequence of this delay, arrived only just in time, on the very morning of the fatal day. The crisis was averted, and the constitutional establishment of the Church of Scotland at this day is, humanly speaking, the result of that[1] memorable night.

He afterwards became Principal of the University of Edinburgh, and his Latin orations in that post made his hearers fancy themselves transported to the Forum of ancient Rome. Four times in eleven years he was Moderator of the General Assembly, and by his calm words in that chair the clergy of the Church of Scotland were induced to acquiesce in the Act of Union. It was during the animosity which he

[1] The accuracy of the story has been doubted; but, as far as can be ascertained, without any adequate grounds.

incurred on that occasion that his colleague in Greyfriars' Church, of which he was the minister, who was violently opposed to the Union, made a fierce attack upon him on the morning of a certain Sunday on which Carstairs was to preach in the afternoon. Whilst this attack was going on, the eyes of the whole congregation were fixed on Carstairs, who, with great composure, began to turn over the leaves of his Bible. In the afternoon a vast concourse assembled to hear him, when he gave out for his text, "Let the righteous smite me, it will not break my bones;" in which he took occasion to vindicate his colleague from any want of regard for him; that, as he knew the "uprightness of his colleague's intention and the goodness of his heart, he was determined to consider any rebuke directed to himself from that place as the strongest expression of his love." It need not be said that congregation and colleague were alike vanquished.

A like instance of his kindly temper is recorded by the younger Calamy, as having occurred on an occasion when he was present in the General Assembly. An old gentleman in the most insulting tone had attacked Carstairs. "I, sir, am as good a man as yourself; bating that you have a sprinkling of court holy water to which I must own myself a stranger. I tell you again, sir, you shall withdraw, or we'll go no further."[1] To which Carstairs, "with great meekness," replied: "'Dear brother, I can more easily forgive this peevish sally of yours than you perhaps will be able to forgive yourself when you come to reflect upon it,' and so withdrew. The

[1] Calamy's *Life*, ii. 159.

matter in dispute was soon determined by the Assembly, but the angry old gentleman could not rest without asking the pardon of his generous foe."

This fine good-humor pervaded all the relations of life. When Calamy told him the insight which he had acquired into the practices of the General Assembly, he cried out: "Verily, to spy out our nakedness are you come; and had you spent ever so much time in contriving a way to discover all our defects at once, you could not have fixed on one more effectual." "One thing," says Calamy, "which gave a peculiar relish to any intercourse with the College at Edinburgh was the entire freedom and harmony between the Principal and the Masters, they expressing a veneration for him as for a common father, and he a tenderness for them as though they had been his children. Were it so in all societies of that sort," adds Calamy, "they would be much more likely to answer the ends of their institution, than by running into wranglings and contentions, and harboring mutual jealousies and suspicions."

When Calamy was attacked, and not without ground, for the latitude of a sermon which he had preached on the importance of being contented with the name of "Christian," without pretending to make any addition, by which in reality they would take from it, it was Carstairs who, with "great mildness and prudence," replied to the fanatic who had assaulted him.[1]

It may be well to fill up the outline of the public life of Carstairs by some touching private incidents. When he was imprisoned in the castle at Edinburgh,

1 Calamy, ii. 179.

a little boy of twelve years old, son of Erskine of Cambo, Governor of the castle, in the course of his rambles through the court, came to the grate of Carstairs' apartment. As he always loved to amuse himself with children, he went to the grate and began a conversation. The boy was delighted, and every day came to the prison-grate — told him stories, brought him provisions, took his letters to the post, was unhappy if Carstairs had no errand to send and no favor to ask. When Carstairs was released, they parted with tears on both sides. One of the first favors that Carstairs asked of King William was that he would bestow the office of Lord Lyon on his young friend, to whom he had owed so much; and he obtained it, with the additional compliment that it should be hereditary in the family. So in fact it continued, till it was unfortunately forfeited by the engagement of Erskine's eldest son in the rebellion of 1745.

Another story illustrates the freshness and simplicity of his pastoral character, amongst the absorbing public affairs which occupied him. His sister, the wife of a Fifeshire clergyman, had become a widow. Carstairs had just arrived in Edinburgh from London, to transact business with King William's ministers. She came over to Edinburgh and went to his lodgings. They were crowded with the nobility and officers of state; and she was told she could not see him. "Just whisper," said she to the servant, "that I desire to know when it would be convenient for him to see me." He returned for answer, "*Immediately*," left the company, came to her, and most affectionately embraced her. On her attempting to apologize,

"Make yourself easy," he said; "these gentlemen are come hither, not on my account, but their own. They will wait with patience till I return. You know I never pray long." And so, after a short fervent prayer, suited to her circumstances, he fixed the time for seeing her more at leisure, and returned in tears to the company.

Towards the ejected Episcopalian clergy he acted with the utmost tenderness and consideration. Two striking instances are recorded. He had a visit from one of them, of the name of Cadell. Carstairs observed with pain that his clothes were threadbare. He eyed him narrowly, and begged him to call again, on the pretext of business, in two days. Meanwhile, he had ordered a suit of clothes from his tailor, to suit not his own but Cadell's make. When Cadell arrived, he found Carstairs in a furious passion at his tailor for mistaking his measure, so that neither coat, waistcoat, nor breeches would sit upon him. Then, turning to Cadell, "They are lost if they don't fit some of my friends; and, by the by, I am not sure but they may answer you." Cadell tried them. They were sent to his lodgings. On putting them on, he found in one of the pockets a ten-pound note, which he immediately brought back. "By no means," said Carstairs. "It cannot belong to me, for when you got the coat you acquired a right to everything in it."

When the great Churchman passed away in full age, he was interred with all honor in the venerable grave-yard of his own church of Greyfriars. As the second founder of the Presbyterian Church was laid in his grave, two mourners were observed to turn aside and burst into tears. They were two Episcopal Nonjurors, whose families for years he had supported.

The grave is unmarked by any monument. The name of Carstairs belonged to no party, English or Scottish. It is not famous among the zealots on either side the Border. But there is none of which the whole ecclesiastical profession ought to be more proud. There is none which more completely rebuts the one-sided accusations of Mr. Buckle against the Church of Scotland. There is none which I commend more warmly to the grateful memory of the Scottish people, or to his successors, whether as Moderators of the General Assembly or as Principals of the College of Edinburgh.

It is not surprising that, after the troubles of the Union were over, the school which had carried the Church of Scotland safely through that crisis, and which numbered amongst its followers such names as Leighton, Charteris, and Carstairs, should have been in the ascendant. The old leaven of the Covenanting, Calvinistic system still continued, but it was more and more subdued, and when it did appear vented itself rather in indignant protests and secessions than in the actual government of the Church.

When Calamy visited Scotland in 1703, "that which he took to be most remarkable was that not one in all the General Assembly was for the Divine right of the Presbyterian form of Church government, though they submitted to it."[1] What a defection in the eyes of the anti-Prelatic anti-Erastian suffering remnant! what an advance in the eyes of all enlightened Christians!

[1] Calamy, vol. ii. p. 153.

It was now that, in the midst of those narrow prejudices which have given rise to Mr. Buckle's impeachment, there sprung up within the Church of Scotland a body of clergy, who, for cultivation and enlightenment, were second to none in Christendom. When Warburton contemptuously said of the Scottish clergy that they were "half of them fanatics and half infidels," he was merely expressing, with the insolent contempt with which high English ecclesiastics have sometimes spoken of other churches, the fact that, side by side with the religious fervor of Scotland, there existed a liberality as conspicuous.[1] Even under the fanaticism of the Covenanters there lay a deep-seated reverence, as we have seen, that the English Church would have done well to recognize in its own Nonconforming members; and what Warburton thought infidelity was the growth of that free and open inquiry which, more than any single cause, kept Christianity alive and respected in England and Scotland during the last century, whilst it was perishing on the Continent. I have spoken of the absence of any eminent work on specially theological subjects emanating from the Scottish clergy. But this deficiency was wonderfully counterbalanced by their extraordinary activity in the general walks of knowledge.

The literary Clergy.

"I must confess," said Dr. Alexander Carlyle in

[1] The same sentiment is expressed more at length in Warburton's Letter to Dr. John Erskine. (See Sir H. Moncrieff Wellwood's *Life of Erskine*, pp. 55, 56. Home once said partly in play to Hume, the historian, that the cause of the fall of a banker's chief clerk, who had appropriated a considerable sum of money, was the books he was in the habit of reading. "What books?" asked the philosopher. "Boston's *Fourfold State* and Hume's *Essays*." Mackenzie's *Life of Home*, p. 22.

1747,[1] on the question of the augmentation of poor livings, "that I do not love to hear this Church called a poor Church, or the poorest Church in Christendom. . . . . I dislike the language of whining and complaint. We are rich in the best goods a church can have — the learning, the manners, and the character of its members. There are few branches of literature in which the ministers of this Church have not excelled. There are few subjects of fine writing in which they do not stand foremost in the ranks of authors, which is a prouder boast than all the pomp of the hierarchy. . . . . Who have written the best histories ancient and modern? It has been clergymen of the Church of Scotland. Who has written the clearest delineation of the human understanding and all its powers? A clergyman of this Church. Who has written the best system of rhetoric, and exemplified it by his own writing? A clergyman of this Church. Who wrote a tragedy that has been deemed perfect? A clergyman of this Church. Who was the most perfect mathematician of the age in which he lived? A clergyman of this Church. . . . . Let us not complain of poverty. It is a splendid poverty indeed. It is *paupertas fœcunda virorum*."

This was a noble boast, and it is well borne out by the brilliant galaxy of names that adorned the chairs and pulpits of Edinburgh in the middle and the close of the last century. Not till quite our own generation have poetry, philosophy, and history found so natural a home in the clergy of England as they did then in the clergy of Scotland. Robert Watson, the historian of Philip II.; Adam Fergusson,[2]

[1] Grub, iv. 155.

[2] For a lively description of Fergusson, see Lord Cockburn's *Memoirs*, p. 48.

the historian of Rome; John Home, the author of the tragedy of "Douglas"; Hugh Blair, the author of the celebrated "Sermons" and of the "Lectures on Rhetoric"; Robert Henry, the philosophic author of the "History of Great Britain";[1] and, lastly and chiefly, William Robertson, the historian of Scotland, of America, and of Charles V., were all ministers of the Church of Scotland. It is a striking tribute to the eminence of the Scottish clergy of that epoch, that when Guy Mannering casts his eyes over the letters of introduction which Pleydell had given him to the first literary characters in Edinburgh, three at least were ministers.

Home.

Of these eminent men, Home may perhaps be considered to have passed voluntarily from his ecclesiastical to his literary career.[2] But of the others, their ecclesiastical career cannot be parted from their literary eminence. No other sermons in Great Britain have been followed by so splendid a success as the once famous, now forgotten, discourses of Hugh Blair. Neither of Tillotson nor of Jeremy Taylor in past times, nor of Arnold or Newman or even Frederick Robertson in our own time, can it be recorded, as of Blair, that they were translated into almost all the languages of Europe, and won for their author a public reward from the Crown. Nor was it only the

Blair.

1 For an amusing account of Dr. Henry's last days, see Lord Cockburn's *Memoirs*, p. 51.

2 The fight which was fought over the tragedy of *Douglas*, and the comparative victory which he won, may be regarded as a decided step in the liberties of the Church of Scotland. When Mrs. Siddons came to Edinburgh not fifty years afterwards, the General Assembly adjourned its sittings that its ministers might attend the theatre. Grub, iv. 83.

vulgar public that was satisfied. Even the despot of criticism (fastidious judge, zealous High-churchman, fanatically English as he was), the mighty Samuel Johnson, who had a few years before declared that no Scottish clergyman had written any good work on religious subjects, pronounced, after his perusal of Blair's first sermon, "I have read it with more than approbation — to say it is good is to say too little."[1] "If they are like the first, they are *sermones aurei, ac auro magis aurei*. I had the honor of first finding and first praising his excellences. I did not stay to add my voice to that of the public."[2] "A noble sermon," he exclaimed of another; "I wish Blair would come over to the Church of England." "I love Blair's sermons, though the dog is a Scotchman and a Presbyterian, and everything he should not be. I was the first to praise him — such is my candor. . . . Let us ascribe it to my candor and his merit."

Robertson.

What Dr. Robertson did for history it is difficult for us, with the advances made since his time, fully to comprehend. It is only when we look on what preceded his works that we are astonished at the comprehensive grasp, the dignity, the learning with which, first of his countrymen, he rose to the height of that great argument. Yet how little do those who know of him as the familiar historian of Charles V. think of him as for many years the mighty Churchman who ruled the Church of Scotland as no one had done since the death of Carstairs. "Those two doctors," said Johnson, speaking of him and Blair, "are wise men and good

[1] Boswell, iii. 459, 467. [2] Ibid. iv. 68.

men."[1] His first appearance was as a young minister in the General Assembly, where he at once led them captive by his eloquence. From that time for twenty years he remained its complete master. His administration was remarkable as showing how complete independence of worldly influence may be combined with complete vindication of the superiority of the law to ecclesiastical caprices. He insisted on the same strictness in the judicial proceedings of the Assembly as was observed in the other courts of justice, and left behind him a series of decisions which were long venerated as a kind of common law in Scotland.

He was also as thorough a Latitudinarian as Leighton. "The first thing," said Lord Elibank, "that gave me a good opinion of you, Dr. Robertson, was your saying, while parties ran high soon after 1745, that you did not think worse of a man's moral character for his having been in rebellion. This was venturing to utter a liberal sentiment while both sides had a detestation of each other." "Dr. Johnson," said Dr. Robertson to the old champion of orthodoxy when they met in London, "allow me to say that in one respect I have the advantage of you. When you were in Scotland you would not come to hear any of our preachers; whereas, when I come here I attend your public worship without scruple, and indeed with great satisfaction."[2]

"Who is Mr. Hayley?" he writes to Gibbon; "his Whiggism is so bigoted and his Christianity so fierce that he almost disgusts one with two very good things."[3]

1 Boswell, iii. 93. 2 Ibid. iv. 196. 3 Gibbon's *Letters*, ii. 251.

He exhibited the singular spectacle of the leader of the Presbyterian Church advocating the relaxation of the penal laws against the Roman Catholics, whilst a nonjuring divine, who afterwards became a bishop, Abernethy Drummond, was active in opposing it.[1] He foretold the time when the whole question of subscription to the existing Confessions would occupy the mind of the Church, and though he could not see his way to a solution of the problem, he never, even in the plenitude of his power or of his years, used any effort to prevent it. And, as he stood at the head of the intellectual and ecclesiastical life of Scotland, so his individual character was not unworthy of such eminence. We still are allowed in his declining years to follow "the pleasant-looking old man, with an eye of great vivacity and intelligence, a large projecting chin, a small hearing trumpet fastened by a black ribbon to a button-hole of his coat, and a large wig powdered and curled" — helping the boys to feed their rabbits on the green, or feasting them with cherries from his favorite tree, or watching the blossoms of the fruit which he was not to see.[2] And when he was laid in his grave in Greyfriars' Church-yard, he was honored by the noblest of all testimonies — a eulogy from a rival in the Church, with whom for long years he had contended but never quarreled. It describes the very model of ecclesiastical statesmanship, the true Archbishop of the Church of Scotland."[3]

1 Grub, iv. 142.

2 Cunningham, ii. 550.

3 It is quoted at length in Grub, iv. 144. It is recorded by his celebrated grandson, Lord Brougham (*Life*, i. 27), that on November 5, 1788, he heard Dr. Robertson preach on the occasion of the centenary of the English Revolution a sermon "of singular and striking

There is another less eminent theologian, but whose work is of extraordinary interest, not so much from its intrinsic merits as from the singular illustration which it affords of the rare liberality of the Scottish clergy at this time. I refer to the "Treatise on Miracles," in answer to David Hume, by Dr. George Campbell, of Aberdeen. It is not too much to say that the name of Hume was, and is still, one of the chief objects of theological terror — not only in Great Britain, but in Europe. Hume was the great skeptic of a skeptical age. But if so good a judge as Adam Smith could say of him that he was the "most perfectly wise and virtuous man he had ever known," it is worthy the consideration of Christian ministers to ponder well before they treat such a character as an enemy of religion. Nor did he put himself forward as an unbeliever. "I am no Deist — I do not so style myself; neither do I desire to be known by that appellation."[1] He

Campbell and Hume.

interest from the extreme earnestness, the youthful fervor, with which it was delivered." It is yet more interesting as a proof of his liberal sentiments, if it be true that it was filled with allusions to the approach of another Revolution, to "the events then passing on the Continent, which would produce an event which our neighbors would ere long have to celebrate like to that which had then called them together;" his boundless exultation in contemplating "the deliverance of so many millions of so great a nation from the follies of arbitrary government." I have received a confirmation of the story from another grandson, Mr. William Robertson, of Kinloch Moidart.

[1] Boswell, i. 255. A like story is told of his speech to Peter Boyle, who called on him after his mother's death, and found him sitting over the fire. "Do you really think, David, that there is nothing more left of her than in those ashes." "Peter," said Hume, laying his hand on his friend's knee, "you very much mistake my opinions if you ascribe to me anything of the kind." I venture to repeat this story as it was once repeated to me from an authentic source, in a form somewhat more lively and likely than that in which it is usually

was constant in his attendance at the worship of the Church,[1] and he presents a delicacy of expression on religious subjects which, even if prudential, stood in remarkable contrast with many of the contemporary scoffers both in England and on the Continent. His reward was that the graces of his character were acknowledged by the clergy even more readily than by the laity. The two Primates of England and Ireland were alone amongst their countrymen in encouraging him to prosecute his history. In his own country he lived on the most intimate terms with the leading clergy of Edinburgh. Blair openly defended him from attacks which he believed to be unjust. The General Assembly[2] steadily refused, though hard pressed, to censure his writings. The works of his friend Lord Kaimes, although an elder, were not even noticed by that body. The crowning example of Christian courtesy was shown by Dr. Campbell. Before publishing his treatise he submitted it to Hume's perusal, and at once accepted his great adversary's criticisms on passages in which the meaning of the controverted word had been misunderstood, or which needed to be softened. Hume himself gracefully acknowledged the urbanity of this truly Christian controversialist.[3] The whole transaction is a green oasis in the history of polemics, and was of itself sufficient to redeem the Scottish clergy from the indiscriminating charges which, with an ignorance surprising in such a man, Mr. Buckle brought against them.

given from Dr. Carlyle. See Burton's *Life of Hume*, i. 294.)

1 Burton's *Hume*, ii. 453.

2 Ibid. ii. 430.

3 Cunningham, ii. 507, 515.

It is in the Established Church that these eminent men found their home. The narrower spirits of the age took refuge in one secession after another in pursuance of the principles indicated in my previous lecture. Yet there are two striking exceptions which show how the generous principles nurtured within the Establishment extended to some of the communities which broke off from it.

One such is the separation commonly called *the Relief.* Gillespie of Carnock stands almost alone amongst the founders of Scottish schisms in having been driven out of the Church rather than voluntarily retiring from it. The word "Relief" expressed all that he needed; and that "Relief," according to the somewhat stern rule of external discipline established by Dr. Robertson, was not granted to him. With the close atmosphere of the Secession he had no sympathy. When condemned by the Assembly he replied in words which are a model of dignified and temperate submission: "Moderator, I desire to receive this sentence of the General Assembly of the Church of Scotland pronounced against me with real concern and awful impressions of the divine conduct in it; but to me I rejoice that it is given not only to rejoice in the name of Christ but also to suffer for it." He heaped no calumnies on the Church after his deposition. In his first sermon preached in the open fields he expressed his hope that no public disputes would ever be the burden of his preaching, but Jesus Christ and Him crucified. "He desired at all seasons to have in his eye that the *wrath of man worketh not the righteousness of God,* and then went on to speak of

The Relief.

Gillespie.

the great truths of the Gospel without one reflection on what had passed."

He still loved the Church from which he had parted, and rather than seek assistance elsewhere, resolved to take his whole work upon himself. The coldness of the Church towards him was a hard return; yet to the end he remained faithful to his first love, and on his death-bed recommended his congregation to "reseek communion with it." The "Relief" has now been absorbed into the United Presbyterians. May we not trace in the gentler and freer spirit which at times appears in that body the traces of the first originator of one of its component parts — the latitudinarian, moderate, Christian-minded Gillespie?

There was yet one other Scottish sect of this period which in a different form exhibited something of the same enlarged temperament. Alone of all the secessions that of John Glasse was not based upon the Covenant but rather on a protest against it. Alone of all Scottish seceders he founded his theology not on the likeness of Christianity to Judaism but on its unlikeness. Extravagant as some of his tenets were, yet his conception of the Church as a purely spiritual community had in it a germ of eternal truth not to be found in the hierarchical pretensions of the other seceders; and the restoration of ancient Christian usages, fantastic as they were, had at least the merit of consistency. Alone in western Christendom this little sect has retained the undoubtedly primitive and once Catholic usages of weekly communions, of love feasts, of the kiss of charity, of washing one another's feet, of abstain-

Glasse.

ing from things strangled, and from blood. It is much to the honor of the General Assembly that they long bore with the eccentricities of this child-like reformer; and in his case they adopted a precedent which, though harsh in its application, contained a principle full of forethought and kindly feeling. Whilst withholding from him the office of minister of the Established Church, they distinctly recognized him as a minister of the Gospel.[1] In this unattached and inoffensive attitude he continued to act. His son-in-law, Sandeman, continued his teaching, and the simple unostentatious piety of this singular Scottish communion has been rewarded in our days by enrolling and retaining amongst its members the most illustrious and the most religious of modern philosophers, Michael Faraday.

Sandeman.

There was no doubt a repressive tendency, a natural revulsion from the extravagance of the former generation, such as the stern rule of Robertson and the shrewd worldly sense of men like Alexander Carlyle unduly fostered. One example of the intolerance which is at times found in the most tolerant of schools appears in the earlier history of the Scottish Latitudinarians; and if the popular view of it may be taken as correct, is too striking to be passed over by any impartial observer.

Intolerance of the Moderates.

In the venerable cemetery of Greyfriars' Church, which contains the dust of all the contending factions of Scottish history — where the monument of the Covenanters recounts their praises almost within sight of the Grassmarket where they died; where rest the noblest leaders both of the

Sir George Mackenzie.

1 Cunningham, ii. 455.

moderate and of the stricter party — there rises another stately monument, at once the glory and the shame of Scottish Liberals. It is the ponderous tomb, bolted and barred, of Sir George Mackenzie, the Lord Advocate under James II.[1] He it is of whom Davie Deans has said that "he will be kenned by the name of Bloody Mackenzie so long as there 's a Scot's tongue to speak the word." He it is whom Wandering Willie saw in that terrible scene — the masterpiece of Scott's genius — of the revels of the old persecutors in the halls of Hell. "There was the Bloody Advocate Mackenzie, who for his worldly wit and wisdom had been to the rest as a god." At the massive wooden doors of that huge mausoleum in the Greyfriars' Church-yard, even to this day we are told that the boys of the old town of Edinburgh venture as a feat of boyish audacity in the gloaming to shout through the key-hole, and then fly for their lives : —

> "Lift the sneck and draw the bar,
> Bloody Mackenzie come out if ye dare."

The strange and instructive aspect of this sinister and blood-stained memory is that it belongs to one who was deemed, even by his political adversaries, "the brightest Scotsman of his time," who was a bold advocate of the rights of the subject, a reformer of some of the worst abuses of Scottish law, and a philosophic theologian of the largest type. "It is in religion as in heraldry," he said ; "the simpler the bearing is, it is so much the purer and the ancienter."

[1] I derive my impressions of George Mackenzie from the hostile but candid and able essay in the *Contemporary Review* of August, 1871, by A. Taylor Innes.

"I am none of those who acknowledge no temples but in their own heads. To chalk out the bordering lines of the Church militant is beyond the geography of my religion." He was perfectly indifferent to the claims of Episcopacy and Presbytery. The laws of his country were for him a sufficient warrant for the forms of religion. Yet this great lawyer, so just, so enlightened beyond his age, was by stress of circumstance, and partly by the excess of his philosophic indifference, induced to frame and administer those dreadful laws by which the Scottish Covenanters were tortured, exiled, and slaughtered. He remains a warning to all liberal statesmen and divines that liberality of theory does not always carry with it liberality of action.

When I stand in that historic cemetery before the tomb of the ancient Covenanters my heart glows with respect for honorable though mistaken adversaries. When I seek for the grave of Carstairs, or gaze on the tomb of Robertson, I delight in the thought that spirits so generous and so noble as theirs were fellow-workers and forerunners in the mission which I and those with whom I labor delight to honor. But when I turn to the monument of the Bloody Mackenzie, it is with the bitter thought that I see there the memorial of a valued friend, who has betrayed and disgraced a noble cause, and given occasion, it may be, to the enemies of freedom, charity, and truth to blaspheme those holy names.

The deviations from the true moderation of the Church of Scotland, which marked the history of Sir George Mackenzie, no doubt appeared from time to time in the later periods which

Controversies respecting:

we have been considering. And it was assisted by the continued inheritance of the old Covenanting leaven, without which the Church would not have been the Church of Scotland, and which maintained its hold on the General Assembly through what was called the "popular party." The cruel execution of Thomas Aikenhead, and the decree of the General Assembly against what were absurdly called the "*atheistical* opinions" of "the *Deists*," blackens the same page of Scottish history that is brightened by "the Act for the settling of schools."[1] It was this same persecuting spirit which, at a later period, as we have seen, attempted, but in vain, to condemn Home, and Kaimes, and Hume; which endeavored to cast out the less known but still highly-interesting names of Simson and Leechman. They were all accused of heresy, and they were all treated leniently, if not acquitted, by the Assembly. Simson's case was the most complicated, and involved the longest controversy. But the two Wisharts and Leechman are again examples, like Leighton and Charteris, of the union of the purest and most elevated religion with free and large speculation. Wishart, who was an ardent admirer of the most saintly of English Latitudinarians,[2] Whichcote, was accused of having diminished the "due weight and influence of arguments taken from the awe of future rewards and punishments;" also of "wishing to remove confessions, and freeing persons from subscribing thereto," and for "licen-

Aikenhead;

Simson;

Wishart;

1 Macaulay, iv. 584. Cunningham, ii. 313.

2 See Principal Tulloch's interesting essay on Benjamin Whichcote, in the *Contemporary Review* of November, 1871.

tiously extending the liberty of Christian subjects." It is of his brother George that Henry Mackenzie has said: "His figure is before me at this moment. It is possible some who hear me may remember him. Without that advantage, I can faintly recall his sainted countenance — that physiognomy so truly expressive of Christian meekness, yet in the pulpit often lighted up with the warmest devotional feeling. In the midst of his family it beamed with so much patriarchal affection and benignity, so much of native politeness graced with those manners which improve its form without wasting its substance, that I think a painter of the apostolic school could have found no more perfect model." Wishart was acquitted, both by the Synod and General Assembly, in 1745.[1]

Leechman.

Leechman was Professor of Divinity at Glasgow. He was in appearance like an ascetic monk; a man distinguished alike for his primitive and apostolic manners, his love of literature, and his liberal opinions. The ground of attack against him was a philosophic sermon on prayer. The Assembly acquitted him in words as honorable to itself as to him: "We have seen, on the one hand, the beauty of Christian charity, and the condescension to remove offense; on the other, the readiness to make all satisfaction."[2]

Lukewarmness.

It is perhaps another form of the almost inevitable onesidedness of each of the great movements of the human mind that, during the ascendency of the Moderates, the Church of Scotland partook of the lukewarmness of zeal in behalf of great religious and philanthropic objects which per-

1 Cunningham, ii. 373–400, 469.

2 Ibid. ii. 469.

vaded all Christendom during the eighteenth century. Yet, in justice both to Scotland and to that now unduly depreciated age, it must be remembered that then, for the first time, were set on foot endeavors seriously to evangelize and enlighten the outlying districts of the Highlands, which, during the fierce contentions for and against the Covenant, had been left untouched, in the depths of ignorance and superstition. Even the system of parochial education, the peculiar glory of the Scottish Church and nation, which had been foreshadowed in the wise schemes of Knox, was first put in force after the settlement of the Revolution.[1]

Reception of Whitefield:

And if we ask for the more stirring signs of religious revival, it can hardly be said that Scotland, during the last century, fell behind England, nor the Established Church of Scotland behind the seceding sects. It is true that when Wesley crossed the Border he found a want of that cordial response which he had found in many parts of his own country. He was too English — must I say, too Arminian, too Oxonian — to rouse the sympathies of the North. But even he, when in 1736, in the far distant Darien, he lighted on the Scottish settlement, after bitter complaints of hearing an extemporary prayer, and of there being public service only once a week, adds, "Yet it must be owned that in all instances of personal or social duty this people utterly shames our countrymen. In sobriety, industry, frugality, patience, in sincerity and openness of behavior, in justice and mercy of all kinds, being not content with exemplary kindness and friendliness to

[1] Cunningham, ii. 314.

one another, but extending it to the utmost of their ability to every stranger that comes within their gates."[1]

By the Seceders;

And when Whitefield came to Scotland it was not, as we have seen, in the seceding Churches, but in the Established Church, that he found his chief support,—if not support, at least toleration.[2] It was from the Church of the Moderates, not from the Church of the Covenant, nor that of the Episcopalians, that three thousand communicants went forth to receive the Holy Eucharist from what the Seceders called the "foul prelatic hands" of the English clergyman.[3] In the West, his chief supporter was no wild fanatic, but a learned, unostentatious scholar, a slow, cautious, and prudent parish minister, M'Culloch of Cambuslang. In the East, the support which had been denied him by Ebenezer Erskine was gladly given by the leader of the popular party—Webster[4]—who, whatever may have been his short-comings, and however much he may have been in some respects opposed to the leaders of the Moderate school, has not only the glory of having forwarded the mission of the English en-

By the Established Church.

1 Wesley's MS. *Journal*, communicated by the kindness of Dr. Rigg.

2 Whitefield called himself "a *moderate* Catholic clergyman of the Church of England." Gledstone's *Whitefield*, p. 496.

3 Gledstone, p. 292.

4 Webster well illustrates the general influence of the Moderates. No doubt he was in the purely technical sense of the word what would be called "the opposition" to the school of Robertson. But not only the words here cited, but his whole intercourse with Dr. Carlyle and the whole attitude towards the Established Church make him a liberal, a humanizing influence, such as would have been vainly sought in the ascendency either of the Covenanters, or even of that party to which in a political and temporary sense Webster belonged. See for his position especially Dr. Somerville's *Memoirs*, pp. 102–107.

thusiast, but of having summed up the whole proceeding with those golden words, which no mere enthusiast could have conceived or penned: "I shall conclude with observing that the grave opposition made to this Divine work by several good men through misinformation or mistaken zeal, and the slippery precipice on which they now stand, may teach us that it is indeed a dangerous thing to censure without inquiry. It may serve likewise as a solemn warning against a party spirit which so far blinds the eyes. It also gives a noble opportunity for the exercise of our Christian sympathy towards these our erring brethren . . . . and should make us long for a removal to the land of vision above . . . . where are no wranglings, no strivings about matters of faith, and where the whole scheme of present worship being removed we shall no more see darkly as through a glass, but face to face, where perfect light will lay a foundation for perfect harmony and love. It is with peculiar pleasure that I often think how my good friend Ebenezer shall then enter into the everlasting mansions with many glorified saints, whom the Associate Presbytery have now given over as the property of Satan. May they soon see their mistake; and may we yet altogether be happily united in the bonds of peace and truth." This is Moderation, if ever there was such on earth. This was in the very depth of the eighteenth century, at the very moment when the Moderate party were beginning to establish their sway. When we are taught to think of the Edinburgh of that age as cold and dead, let us remember that it was of it that Whitefield, when he left it, exclaimed, "O Edinburgh, Edinburgh, I think I shall never forget thee!" And that same Edinburgh never forgot him. When, years afterwards, he came to the Scottish capital again, he was in danger of being hugged to death by the enthusiastic reception of its citizens, and he sat, it is said, amongst them, "like a king of men on his throne." When, yet later, two months after his death, Foote endeavored to bring out a play in ridicule of his eccentricities, the town indignantly rose, and the pulpits of the Established Church rang with earnest rebukes.[1]

The balance which was held thus evenly in the last century, at the beginning of this was disturbed; and two memorable convulsions undermined the hitherto strong position of the Moderate party in the Church of Scotland. One was the contest for the chair of mathematical professor between Macknight and Leslie. On that occasion the Moderate clergy, the descendants of Robertson and Blair, were found, from a fatal mixture of party and professional spirit, ranged on the side of ignorance and bigotry; and the Popular clergy, the descendants of Rutherford and Thomas Boston, from a combination of political strategy with hereditary animosity against their ancient enemies, were found as champions of science and freedom.

Macknight and Leslie.

The other was the occasion when, from the union of these two discordant forces, the Church of Scotland drove from its ranks the brightest genius and the most philosophical and most spiritual divine that had for many years adorned its clergy — Edward Irving and John M'Leod Campbell.

Irving and M'Leod Campbell.

1 Gledstone's *Whitefield*, pp. 477, 499.

Into these and the yet more strange controversies that followed I decline to enter. The fires of the Disruption still glow too warmly, even in its ashes, to allow a stranger to walk boldly among them. But they may be watched from a distance, amidst the lights and shadows thrown upon them from the past, and from the hopes of a brighter future, which I reserve for my next lecture.

NOTE.

IN treating the somewhat complex aspect of the Church of Scotland during the last century, it may be well to repeat briefly the position already indicated. It was not my intention to enter into the detailed questions at issue between the "Moderate" and the "Popular" party; but to describe the general influence of the spirit of moderation over the whole Church. The name of "Moderate," like all other party names, has been used as a term of reproach equally for the best and the worst of men; and it was therefore my object, as far as possible, to abstain from employing it in this technical and at the same time indiscriminate sense. It is clear that, in point of fact, the Church of Scotland at large was as proud of the leaders of its public opinion in the eighteenth century, as the seceding sections of the Church are now anxious to disparage them. It is sufficient to contrast the contemptuous expressions used by modern partisans, with the cordial and generous tribute of one whose very name is a guarantee for strictness of life and faith. "The names of such men as Cuming and Wishart and Walker and Dick and Robertson and Blair, are embalmed, with the name of Erskine, in the hearts of all who have learned, in any manner, how to value whatever has been most respectable in our Zion. God grant that, while their memory is yet fresh in the mind, the men who fill their places in the world may catch a portion of their spirit! God grant that while they, like Elijah of old, may yet seem to be dropping their mantle on the earth, their spirit also, like that of the prophet, may yet remain to bless the children of men."[1] This was the feeling towards the leading "Moderates" expressed by the venerable biographer of the leader of the popular party of that age. It is the very school, whose beneficent influence is portrayed in these glowing terms, which has in recent declarations been described as the "antagonist of the religious life of the Scottish Church," and of which it has been said that "their history was in one word,—'Ruin.'"

1 Sir Henry Moncrieff Wellwood's *Life of Erskine*, p. 481.

LECTURE IV.

THE PRESENT AND THE FUTURE OF THE CHURCH OF SCOTLAND.

DELIVERED BEFORE THE PHILOSOPHICAL INSTITUTE,

JANUARY 12, 1872.

LECTURE IV.

THE PRESENT AND THE FUTURE OF THE CHURCH OF SCOTLAND.

I HAVE almost reached the farthest limits to which I shall have to tax your patience and your forbearance. But I would still venture to say a few words on the future of the Church of Scotland, so far as it can be divined from the moral and religious phases of its former history and of its present condition.

Union of the Church of Scotland.

The question which I would propound is, What germs can we find of unity and prosperity in the discordant elements of which we have been speaking? It will not be supposed that I come here to suggest any details of organic union, such as have been sometimes proposed between the Free Church and the United Presbyterians, or between the Episcopal and the Presbyterian Churches generally. In such projects of internal administration it becomes not a stranger to intermeddle, and even if it did, the study of the ecclesiastical history of Scotland, as of other countries, would make me hesitate in proposing schemes of union which are often rather military defenses against a common foe than harmonious aspirations after a common good; and which often cannot be effected without effacing peculiarities which are not less valuable than unity itself. When I look on the three estranged sections of Scottish religious life, I fully sympathize with that touching application of Coleridge's beautiful lines, which was made some years ago by a distinguished Moderator of the General Assembly:[1] —

"Alas! they had been friends in youth;
But whispering tongues can poison truth;
Each spake words of high disdain
  And insult to his heart's best brother:
They parted — ne'er to meet again!
  But never either found another
To free the hollow heart from paining;
They stood aloof, the scars remaining,
Like cliffs which had been rent asunder:
  A dreary sea now flows between;
But neither heat, nor frost, nor thunder,
  Shall wholly do away, I ween,
  The marks of that which once hath been."

Nevertheless, the increasing elements of union, which are visible in other Churches, have not failed in Scotland.

It will be remembered that when the lamented Prevost Paradol addressed the audience of Edinburgh a few years ago, he said, in answer to the question of what Church he was an adherent: "I belong to that Church which has no name, but of which the members recognize each other wherever they meet."[2] He meant, no doubt, that fellowship of sentiment which creates a unity amongst all educated men throughout Christendom. It is the intellectual and philosophical expression of a very old theological truth, — that which constitutes the first clause of the twenty-fifth article of the Confession of Faith: "The Catholic or Universal Church, which is invisible, consists of the whole number of

The Spiritual Church of Scotland.

[1] Address of the Rev. Dr. Norman M'Leod, as Moderator of the General Assembly in 1869.

[2] Lectures delivered at Edinburgh in 1869.

the elect which have been, are, or shall be, gathered into one, under Christ, the Head thereof, and is the spouse, the body, the fullness of Him that filleth all in all." These elect spirits, and the influences which they embody, are indeed confined to no one Church or country, but they are the links which draw all Churches and countries together. And it is one of the advantages of our time, as Prevost Paradol observed, that education of itself forms an intellectual unity amongst cultivated men, which, though unknown in the earlier ages of Christian Europe, is now beginning to take its place beside the moral unity already perceived to exist amongst the good men of every time — a communion of sages not indeed coextensive with, but analogous to, the communion of saints.

But what is true of the universal Church and of the general community of the civilized world, is also in a more restricted sense true of the religious communions of particular countries, and especially of Scotland.

The true spiritual Church of Scotland includes them all — with the characteristics common to Scotsmen, but without the dividing characteristics of the several communions. And this union is, as regards the Presbyterians of Scotland, the more easy, because of that singular identity of outward doctrine and ritual of which I have before spoken: "It is a fine saying of a German Professor in his history of the Scottish Church," said one of the noblest of modern Scottish Free Churchmen,[1] "'In Scotland there are no sects, only parties.' He meant that we should

[1] Dr. Duncan, in Knight's *Peripatetica*, p. 36.

not dignify our differences by the name of sects; we are only parties in one great sect — the species of a genus." To all who have been subject to the influence of the religion of Scotland there remains a peculiar flavor derived from no other source; and many might be named of whom the description of the Wanderer in Wordsworth's "Excursion" is literally true: —

> "The Scottish Church, both on himself and those
> With whom from childhood he grew up, had held
> The strong hand of her purity; and still
> Had watched him with an unrelenting eye.
> This he remembered in his riper age
> With gratitude, and reverential thoughts.
> But by the native vigor of his mind,
> By loneliness, and goodness, and kind works,
> Whate'er, in docile childhood or in youth,
> He had imbibed of fear or darker thought
> Was melted all away: so true was this,
> That sometimes his religion seemed to me
> Self-taught, as of a dreamer in the woods;
> Who to the model of his own pure heart
> Shaped his belief as grace divine inspired,
> Or human reason dictated with awe."

I propose to follow out the thought of this larger and more original growth of religion by taking examples from the various communions which shall exhibit the elements of this invisible or spiritual Church of Scotland, not in their disunion, but in their union; and I will conclude by showing what is the bearing of this union on the fortunes of the central institution of the National Church itself.

Let me speak first of the present sentiment prevailing towards the more ancient forms of Christendom. It cannot be doubted that they are now regarded from quite a different point

Antiquarian revival.

of view to that in which they were regarded in Scotland in the sixteenth, the seventeenth, or even the eighteenth century. Scotland has been visited by that revival of antiquarian and mediæval lore which was, in the times of which we have spoken, almost equally distasteful to the spirit of the Covenanters and the spirit of the Moderates. Nay, it may almost be said that in that reaction she has herself borne a principal part. It was Walter Scott, as Carlyle has well described, who gave the chief stimulus to the movement in Great Britain, and the authors of the "Tracts for the Times" claimed him, not without ground, though with a total misconception of his larger and loftier position, as one of its first founders. But this one fact of itself shows that the change of which I speak was altogether independent of any extraneous ecclesiastical influence.

The ritual of the Church of England, which Jenny Geddes or her stool cast out from the Episcopal and Presbyterian Churches alike, has at last gained complete possession of the Episcopal Church, and is here and there making its way even in Presbyterian Churches. The organ, so long regarded as the "kist full of whistles," or even as the Beast of the Apocalypse, has been heard to breathe out its prelatic blasts in more than one of the Established, and even of the Secession Churches.

The architecture of mediæval times has in our later days been copied by every branch of Presbyterianism. The remains of the ancient abbeys are deeply cherished by the spiritual descendants of the Protestant mobs who destroyed them, sometimes even more than by the spiritual descendants of the ancient Catholic chiefs who built them.

Never in the most monastic corner of Canterbury or of Westminster have I found an eye more keen to appreciate or a tongue more ready to express the peculiar charm of Gothic architecture than in an old Scottish sacristan of the parish church of Dunblane, who had never crossed the Border, but was able, with genuine enthusiasm, to point out the delicate proportions, the "perfect window," the historic associations of the venerable cathedral under which his own church was sheltered. Lord Cockburn has commemorated in an epitaph half comical, half tragical, the shoemaker "who was for seventeen years the keeper and shower" of the Cathedral of Elgin; and told how, "whilst not even the Crown was doing anything for its preservation, he, with his own hands, cleared it of many thousand cubic yards of rubbish, disinterring the bases of the pillars, collecting the carved fragments, and introducing order and propriety. Whoso reverences this cathedral will respect the memory of this man." No Dean of Anglican chapter or Roman basilica is more proud of the sacred edifice committed to his charge than is the parish minister of Sweetheart Abbey, amongst the ruins of which he dwells, and whose very stones he delights to honor.

The existence of this wide-spread feeling in the Presbyterian Church is a proof, on the one hand, that however much the Episcopal Communion may assist, it was not needed to create, sentiments and tastes which have grown up indigenously in Scotland itself. It is a proof, on the other hand, that any Scottish Episcopalian who understands the wants of his age and appreciates the feelings of his countrymen, will by the Church of Scotland be received as a brother and a friend. When I said in my first lecture that the future mission of the Episcopal Church was principally to convey English ideas into Scotland, nothing was further from my thoughts than to deny the existence of purely northern Episcopalians. No one knows better than myself how genuine is the Scottish blood which warms many a true Episcopalian heart. It has not been my intention in these lectures to name any living illustrations of my arguments, but in this case I may be permitted to prove the truth of my position by pointing to two dignitaries of the Scottish Church, to whom I refer with the more freedom because I know they are not present, whom I select from their brethren both as furnishing the most undoubted instances of this native Caledonian character in the Episcopal Communion, and as the most significant examples of the general truth which I am endeavoring to enforce.

Larger liberality of Episcopalians.

Is there any single ecclesiastic in Edinburgh who rallies round him a wider amount of genuine Scottish sentiment and brotherly love, than that venerable Dean who is an absolute impersonation of "the reminiscences" of all the Scottish Churches, who in his largeness of heart embraces them all, and in his steadfast friendship, his generous championship of forgotten truths and of unpopular causes, proves himself to be in every sense the inheritor of the noble Scottish name which he so worthily bears?

Dean Ramsey.

And if we look into the wilds of the Highlands, — although it is "a far cry to Loch Awe," — we must bring out from thence one who,

Bishop Ewing.

in all meetings of Anglican or quasi-Anglican prelates, bears witness by his very countenance and appearance to the romantic character which I have before described as the main link in the last century between the Scottish Episcopalian Church and the rest of the nation. There, in the region of Argyll and the Isles, may be seen one who has under his charge the most purely native and unalloyed specimens of hereditary Episcopalians; who, in all the graces and humors of his race, is a Celtic Scotsman to the backbone; who has always, though a Bishop, acknowledged the Christian character of his Presbyterian brethren; who, though a Dissenter, has always borne his testimony against the secularizing influences of the voluntary system of which he is an unwilling victim; who, though a minister of one of the secessions from the Church of Scotland, has always lifted up his voice in behalf of those wider and more generous views, of which the grand old office of Episcopacy was intended to be the depository, and to which, though it has often been unfaithful in Scotland as elsewhere, it may, through such men as those of whom I speak, render the most signal services both in their own sphere and in the Church at large.

I turn to the other sections of religious life, — those which more nearly adhere to the national form of worship, — the various fragments which have at various times broken off from the Established Church, and which I have described as inheriting more than any other the spirit of the ancient Covenanters. No doubt there is a difficulty in bending to any accommodation the stubborn steadfastness which prides itself on isolation, and lives by

Larger moderation of the seceding Churches.

disruption. Often, when we think of them or their forefathers, on the mountain side, or in their hall of assembly, the well-known lines of Milton recur: —

> "Others apart sat on a hill retired,
> . . . . and reasoned high
> Of providence, foreknowledge, will, and fate,
> Fixed fate, free will, foreknowledge absolute,
> And found no end, in wandering mazes lost."

Yet even here there are symptoms of a spirit from another quarter which has broken and will still more break into this retirement.

Even David Deans's doubts "had been too many and too critical to permit him unequivocally to unite with any of the seceders from the National Church. He had ever been a humble pleader for the good old cause without rushing into 'right-hand excesses, divisions, and separations. Even he, after making the necessary distinctions betwixt compliance and defection,' 'holding back and stepping aside,' 'slipping and stumbling,' 'snares and errors,' was brought to the broad admission that each man's conscience would be the best guide for his pilotage, and that in the Established Church his son-in-law might safely find a field for his ministrations; and, on his death-bed, it was only, as May Hettly observed, when 'his head was carried' and his mind wandering that he muttered something 'about national defections, right-hand extremes and left-hand fallings off:' his deliberate expressions were of duty, of humility, and of the full spirit of charity with all men."[1]

In like manner, let us hope that the age of the Disruption has been succeeded by a generation not

[1] *Heart of Mid-Lothian.*

baptized into that fierce fire, and probably there are few now in Scotland who can enter into the violence with which at that time households were rent asunder, children quarreled in the streets, ancient friends parted. Auchterarder, the scene of the original conflict, after a few years settled into a haven of perfect peace; the pastor whose intrusion provoked the collision between the spiritual and civil courts lived and died respected by the whole parish. Many would now join with the honored historian of the catastrophe of 1843 in that truly Christian discourse, in which, whilst vindicating the right of the Free Church[1] to sever itself, he withdrew any claim to its being regarded as a fundamental or essential principle of religion.

There are few who would now speak of a well-intentioned endeavor to reconcile two complex legal claims as an attempt to "hurl the Redeemer from his throne," and "to tear the crown from the Saviour's head;" or who would consider that even occasional attendance at the worship of the Established Church was "a sin," or "its Church meetings as no better than the assembling of so many Mohammedans in a Turkish mosque," or "the parish minister as the one excommunicated man of the district, with whom no one is to join in prayer, whose church is to be avoided as an impure and unholy place, whose addresses are not to be listened to, whose visits are not to be received, who is everywhere to be put under the ban of the community."

These exaggerated expressions of party spirit are

[1] "The Church and its Living Head," a sermon preached on November 13, 1859, by the Rev. John Hanna, LL. D.

worth citing only as water-marks of the tide of bitterness, which has now receded far into the ocean, never more, it may be hoped, to recover the shores which it has left.

On the other hand, the religious fervor, of which the Covenanters and the seceders of various views claim, and perhaps with justice, to be the predominant representatives, has overflowed all the borders of the Churches. The language, no doubt, of Rutherford's Letters and Thomas Boston's "Fourfold State" (as of Bunyan's "Grace Abounding" amongst Englishmen), is now antiquated and distasteful; but the grace and beauty of their devotion is appreciated in a far wider circle than when they lived. And from the revivals of our more modern days, out of the smoke and sulphur of the volcano of the Disruption, two names of the departed emerge of which the main claims consist in those qualities — not which divided them from their brethren, but which brought them together.

Thomas Chalmers.

Every Scottish Churchman, I had almost said every Scotsman, claims, whether before or after 1843, the honored name of Chalmers. To attempt to portray his noble character would be in me as impertinent as for you it would be needless. Yet there are a few words which I would fain utter — the more so, as they are in part suggested by my own humble recollections of that wise and good man. *Virgilium tantum vidi.* Eleven days before his death, in the city of Oxford, for the first and last time, I had the privilege of speaking with Dr. Chalmers. I was too young and too English at that time to be much occupied with the divisions which parted the

Free from the Established Church; and there was assuredly nothing in his appearance or conversation which recalled them. But I was not too young to appreciate, nor am I yet too old to forget, the force, the liveliness, the charity with which he spoke of everything on which he touched. Three points specially have remained fixed in my memory which assuredly betokened a son not of the Covenant, but of the Church universal. He was full of the contrast of the two biographies which he had just finished; one was that of "John Foster," the other of "Thomas Arnold." "Two men," he said, "so good, yet with a view of life so entirely different; the one so severe and desponding, the other so joyous and hopeful." He had completed the perusal of another book, of which it seemed equally strange that he should have through all his long life deferred reading it till that time, and that having so delayed he should then have had the wonderful energy to begin and master it. It was Gibbon's "Decline and Fall;" and the old man's face, Evangelical, devout Scotsman as he was, kindled into enthusiasm as he spoke of the majesty, the labor, the giant grasp displayed by that greatest and most skeptical of English historians. Another spring of enthusiasm was opened when he looked round on the buildings of the old prelatic, mediæval Oxford. "You have the best machinery in the world, and you know not how to use it." Such were the words which are still written, as taken down from his mouth, on the photograph of the University Church in the High Street, which was given to him by his host[1] at that time, which was restored to that host

[1] Henry Acland, now the distinguished Regius Professor of Medicine at Oxford.

by Chalmers's family after his death, and by him given to me when I left Oxford, in recollection of that visit. "You have the best machinery in the world, and you know not how to use it." How true, how discriminating, and how amply justified by the prodigious efforts which, as I trust, since that time Oxford has made to use that good machinery. How unlike to the passion for destruction for destruction's sake which has taken possession of many who use his venerable name in vain! How like to the active, organizing mind, which saw in establishments and institutions of all kinds not lumber to be cast away, but machinery to be cherished and used. In front of that academic church of Oxford we parted, just as he touched on the question of the interpretation of the Apocalypse. "But this," he said, "is too long to discuss here and now; you must come and finish our conversation when we meet at Edinburgh." That meeting never came. He returned home; and the next tidings I had of him was that he was departed out of this world of strife.

As I read his biography that brief conversation rises again before me, and seems the echo of those wider and more generous views which at times were overlaid by the controversies into which he was drawn. Such is his own account of his longing recollection of the earlier days when he lived in the great ideas which are the foundation of all religion.

"O, that He possessed me with a sense of his holiness and his love," he exclaims, after an interval of twenty-six years, "as He at one time possessed me with a sense of his goodness and his power and his pervading agency. I remember," he continues, "when a student of divinity, and long before I could relish evangelical sentiment, I spent nearly a twelvemonth in a sort of mental elysium, and the one idea which ministered to my soul all its rapture was the magnificence of the Godhead and the universal subordination of all things to the one great purpose for which He evolved and was supporting creation. I should like to be so inspired over again, but with such a view of the Deity as coalesced and was in harmony with the doctrine of the New Testament." Such a view he doubtless gained; nor was it, if we may humbly say so, in any way incompatible (if Science and Religion both be true) with that which was the source of his earliest, and, so it would seem, his latest religious fervor.[1]

Even late in life he was accused by suspicious zealots of being an enemy to Systematic Divinity; and his reply was certainly not calculated to allay the alarm. Long did he cling to the freer and nobler views of Theology. "My Christianity," he said most wisely and truly, "approaches nearer to Calvinism than to any of the *isms* in Church history; but broadly as Calvin announces 'truth,' he does not bring it forward in that free and spontaneous manner which I find in the New Testament." The passage from English poetry which he quoted more frequently than any other was that pregnant passage from the Moravian Gambold, which contains within itself the germs of all the broader and higher views of faith:—

"The man
That could surround the sum of things, and spy
The heart of God and secrets of his empire

[1] Hanna's *Life of Chalmers*, iii. 206.

> Would speak but love. With love the bright result
> *Would change the hue of intermediate things,*
> *And make one thing of all theology."*

And even in the very ferment of the Sustentation Fund he could exclaim, "Who cares about the Free Church compared with the Christian good of the people of Scotland? Who cares about any Church, but as an instrument of Christian good? For be assured that the moral and religious well-being of the population is of infinitely higher importance than the advancement of any sect."[1]

John Duncan.

The other departed light of the great movement of 1843, whom I would recall for a moment, is one whom I never met, but whom the descriptions of his friends and disciples place before us in so vivid a light, that one almost seems to have seen him,—in his multifarious learning, in his simple-minded, eccentric detachment from all the cares of this world, almost a Scottish Neander,—I mean Dr. John Duncan. In that charming volume, which gives the most casual, but also the most intimate convictions of his mind, it is remarkable that, to the peculiar doctrines which divide the Free Church from the Established, there is hardly an allusion; that even its peculiar Calvinistic theology and Presbyterian platform occupies a very secondary place. "I am first a Christian, next a Catholic, then a Calvinist, fourthly a Pædo-Baptist, and fifth a Presbyterian." How many would have reversed this order, and even placed before all, "I am a Covenanter; I am a Non-intrusionist." "I suspect," he said, "that, after all, there is only one heresy, and that is Anti-

1 Hanna's *Life of Chalmers*, i. 147, 241, 251; iv. 384, 394.

nomianism." How many there are who think almost everything is heresy except Antinomianism. Again, let us hear him on the progress of theology. "There is a progressive element in all things, and therefore in religion. . . . . It is a mistake to look on the Fathers as our seniors. They are our juniors. The Church has advanced wonderfully since its foundation was laid." Again, let us hear the touching description of an ancient Catholic monument, which implies even more than it says: "There is an old stone cross of granite by the roadside as you wind up the hill at Old Buda in Hungary, upon which a worn and defaced image of our Saviour is cut, which I used often to pass. Below the granite block are the words, 'O vos omnes qui transitis per viam attendite et videte si est ullus dolor sicut dolor meus.' The thorough woebegoneness of that image used to haunt me long — that old bit of granite, the ideal of human sorrow, weakness, and woebegoneness. To this day it will come back before me — always with that dumb gaze of perfect calmness — no complaining — the picture of meek and mute suffering. I am a Protestant and dislike image-worship, yet never can I get that statue out of my mind."[1]

United Presbyterians.

I might follow out these remarks to the other seceding communions. I have already spoken of the finer elements of the Relief and of the Glassites of the "Secession;" I gladly record that their deadly feud with Whitefield was at last suspended. And for the United Presbyterians, it is something to say that they have merged at least one

[1] *Peripatetica* (Reminiscences of Dr. Duncan by his friend and pupil, Dr. Knight).

difference in a common principle. It is still more to say that they have relaxed in some degree the strictness of the obligation which binds the Scottish Churches to the Westminster Confession. It is most of all to say that there are amongst them those who regard freedom of thought as more valuable than freedom of patronage, and that "*Rab and his Friends*," and the "*Horæ Subsecivæ*" represent to all the world the precious gifts which all the Churches equally may long to claim.

Edward Irving.

As I approach the Established Church, I venture to advert to yet a few other names of the dead, which belong to the whole Scottish Church in it widest sense. One is Edward Irving. If by the pressure of an exclusive influence which then preponderated, but has now ceased, within the Scottish Church, he was cast out from its pale — if, partly by his genius, partly by his eccentricities, he soared into regions far removed from it, he was not the less, by nature and by choice, its genuine child. Well it is that he should rest in the crypt of Glasgow Cathedral — that one great religious monument of Scotland which combines in unbroken continuity the age and the youth of her eventful history.

No Scottish, no English divine within our memory, has so nearly succeeded in uniting modern thought with the stately, stiff, elaborate oratory of ancient times. His true teachers were the great writers of a wider range than his own country or communion. Hooker's "Ecclesiastical Polity," found in a farm-house near Annan, was, as he calls it, "the venerable companion of his early years." "I fear not to confess," he said, "that Hooker, Taylor, and Baxter in theology; Bacon and Newton and Locke, in philosophy, have been my companions, as Shakespeare and Spenser and Milton in poetry. I cannot learn to think as they have done — that is the gift of God; but I can teach myself to think as disinterestedly, and to express as honestly what I think and feel." Coleridge was to him "the wise and generous teacher, the good man who had helped an anxious inquirer to the way of truth."[1] His earliest friend and school-fellow was the greatest of living Scottish writers. No words that Thomas Carlyle ever wrote are more full of pathos than those which fell from his pen on hearing of his friend's death. "Edward Irving's career has closed. The spirit of the time which would not enlist him as its soldier must needs in all ways fight against him as its enemy; it has done its part, and he has done his. One of the noblest natures — a man of antique, heroic nature, in questionable modern garniture which he could not wear. But for him I had never known what is meant by the communion of man with man. His was the freest, brotherliest, bravest human soul mine ever came in contact with. I call him, on the whole, the best man I have, after trial enough, found in this world, or now hope to find. . . . The voice of our son of thunder — with its deep tone of wisdom that belonged to all articulate-speaking ages, never inaudible amidst wildest dissonances that belong to this inarticulate age — has gone silent so soon. Closed are those lips. The large heart, with its large bounty, where wretchedness found solacement, and they that were wandering in darkness the light as of

[1] Oliphant's *Life of Irving*, i. 30, 56, 416.

a home, has paused. The strong man can no more; beaten on from without, undermined from within, he must sink overwearied at nightfall, when it was yet but the midseason of day. He was forty-two years and some months old; Scotland sent him forth a Herculean man: our mad Babylon wore and wasted him with her engines, and it took her twelve years. . . . . He died the death of the true and brave. His last words, they say, were 'In life and in death I am the Lord's.' He sleeps with his fathers in that loved birthland. Babylon, with its deafening inanity rages on, but to him innocuous, unheeded forever."[1]

Thomas Erskine.

The mention of Carlyle and Irving suggests another, — a venerable spirit lately removed from us, dear to each of them, dear to many a Scottish heart, — Thomas Erskine of Linlathen. There are not a few to whom that attenuated form and furrowed visage seemed a more direct link with the unseen world than any other that had crossed their path in life. Always on the highest summits at once of intellectual cultivation and of religious speculation, he seemed to breathe the refined atmosphere, —

> "Where the immortal shapes
> Of bright aërial spirits live insphered
> In regions mild of calm and serene air,
> Above the smoke and stir of this dim spot,
> Which men call Earth."

Other loving hands[2] may describe his goings out

1 Carlyle, *Essays*.

2 For the present it may be sufficient to refer to the interesting Preface to "Some Letters of Thomas Erskine," by his friend Bishop Ewing, which contains also the graceful tribute to his memory by Principal Shairp. *Present Day Papers*, pp. 1–66.

and comings in amongst you. But it may be permitted to an English stranger, who knew him only during his later years, to bear this humble testimony to the gift which the Scottish Church in all its branches received in that aged servant of the Lord. I have heard it said that once meeting a shepherd in the Highlands, he said to him, in that tone which combined in so peculiar a manner sweetness and command, and with that penetrating emphasis which drew out of every word that he used the whole depth of its meaning, "Do you know the Father?" and that years afterwards, on those same hills, he encountered that same shepherd, who recognized him, and said, "I know the Father now." The story, whether true or not, well illustrates the hold which the memory of that face and figure and speech had on all who ever came across it. Never shall I forget, on my first visit, the profound pathos with which, in family worship, he read and commented on the 136th Psalm, "Who smote Egypt and his firstborn: for his mercy endureth forever. . . . . Who smote Pharaoh in the Red Sea: for his mercy endureth forever." "Yes," he said, "there was mercy even for Pharaoh; even Egypt and his first-born had a place in the mercy of God;" and then, with the same thought, darting forward to a like stern text of the New Testament: "'Jacob have I chosen, and Esau have I rejected;' yes, but Jacob was chosen for *his* special purpose, and Esau — that fine character — was rejected and preserved for another purpose not less special." "The purpose of God is to make us better. He can have no other intention for us."

No written record can reproduce the effect of conversations, of which the peculiar charm consisted in the exquisite grace with which he passed from the earthly to the heavenly, from the humorous to the serious, from the small things of daily affection to the great things of the ideal world. "The element of the bird is the air; the element of the fish is the water; and the heart of God is Jacob Böhmen's element." This was a favorite quotation of his from the mystical Silesian. "That is true of all of us; we are just fish out of water when we are not living in the heart of God." "What is Christianity? It is the belief in the inexhaustible love of God for man." "He came to seek that which is lost *until He find it.*" "What is human existence? It is not probation, it is education. Every step we take upwards or downwards is a stepping-stone to something else." "What is the proper use of Religion? The sun was made to see by, not to look at."[1] "What is the effect of Revelation to us? It is the disclosure to us of our true relations to God and to one another, as when an exile, after long years' absence, returns home, and sees faces which he does not recognize. But one in whom he can trust comes and says, 'This aged man is your father; this boy is your brother, who has done much for you; this child is your son.'" These and such as these were amongst the sublime thoughts that sustained his soul in what at times might have seemed an almost entire isolation from all ecclesiastical ordinances, but what was, in fact, a

1 This saying he used to cite as one of the best of his esteemed friend Alexander Scott, who was wont to say, in regard to him, "I cannot think of God without thinking of Thomas Erskine." *Present Day Papers*, p. 5.

communion with the inner spirit of all. Presbyterian by his paternal connection with the author of the Institutes and the minister of Greyfriars,[1] Episcopalian by his maternal descent and by his early education, it came to pass that in later life, whilst still delighting in the occasional services and ministrations of the Episcopal Church, and enjoying to the last the tender care of an Episcopalian curate, he yet habitually frequented the worship and teaching of the National Church, both in country and in town — a living proof of the effacement of those boundary lines which, before the exasperations of our latter days, were to many of the best Episcopalians and Presbyterians almost as if they did not exist. In all the varying Scottish communions he had those who counted his friendship one of their chief privileges; and not only there, and in the hearts of loving friends in England, but far away with Catholic Frenchmen in Normandy, and in the bright religious society in which he had dwelt in former days by the distant shores of Geneva, his memory was long cherished, and will not pass away so long as any survive who had seen him face to face.

There are two others, of a far different type, whom I have reserved for the last, because, unlike those whom I have hitherto noticed, their names are known, not only in the contracted circles of a theological atmosphere, not only through the length and breadth of Scotland, but wherever the English tongue

[1] He used to say, in later life, "I greatly value the fixed order of Lessons and Psalms in the Prayer-book"; and then he would add, with his peculiar humor, "and this, I think, is the one single spiritual benefit which I have received from the Church of England."

is spoken, and wherever genius and wisdom are honored, and who are nevertheless completely Scotsmen, completely Scottish Churchmen, in the largest sense; who, though departed from us for a longer space than those I have just named, are still living and present influences; who, in their different measures, can be overlooked in no Scottish ecclesiastical history worthy of the name—I mean Robert Burns and Walter Scott.

Each of these great men represents the several tendencies of which I have spoken,—the Romantic, the Independent, and the Moderate attitude of the Scottish Church. And each justifies his title to be considered not only as a poet, but as a prophet—not only as a delightful companion but as a wise religious teacher.

Robert Burns.

Burns was the Prodigal Son of the Church of Scotland, but he was still her genuine offspring. I have already spoken of "The Cotter's Saturday Night." But this was not all. He who could pen the keen sarcasms of "Holy Willie's Prayer," and the "Address to the Unco' Guid," which pierce through the hollow cant and narrow pretensions of every church in Christendom with a sword too trenchant but hardly too severe, showed that he had not lived in vain in the atmosphere of the philosophic clergy and laity of the last century, whose kindly and genial spirit saved him from being driven by the extravagant pretensions of the popular Scottish religion into absolute unbelief. Much as there may be in these poems that we lament, yet even they retain fragments of doctrine not less truly Evangelical than philosophical.

"Wha made the heart, 'tis He alone
Decidedly can try us,
He knows each chord, its various tone,
Each spring, its various bias:
Then at the balance let 's be mute,
We never can adjust it;
What 's done we partly may compute,
But ken na what 's resistet."

That may perhaps not be the theology of Calvin, but it certainly is the theology of the Sermon on the Mount.

What prayer more comprehensive and more pathetic was ever uttered for a Christian household than that left at the manse where the poet had slept?

"O thou dread Pow'r, who reign'st above!
I know thou wilt me hear:
When for this scene of peace and love
I make my pray'r sincere.

"The hoary sire — the mortal stroke
Long, long, be pleas'd to spare!
To bless his little filial flock,
And show what good men are.

"She, who her lovely offspring eyes
With tender hopes and fears,
O bless her with a mother's joys,
But spare a mother's tears!

"Their hope, their stay, their darling youth,
In manhood's dawning blush;
Bless him, thou God of love and truth,
Up to a parent's wish!

"The beauteous, seraph sister-band,
With earnest tears I pray,
Thou know'st the snares on ev'ry hand,
Guide thou their steps alway!

"When soon or late they reach that coast,
O'er life's rough ocean driv'n,
May they rejoice, no wand'rer lost,
A family in heav'n!"

What advice more profound and more pastoral was ever given as a guide for youth than in the "Epistle to a Young Friend"? —

"I wave the quantum o' the sin,
The hazard o' concealing;
But och! it hardens a' within,
And petrifies the feeling.
. . . . . .

"The fear o' hell's a hangman's whip,
To haud the wretch in order;
But where ye feel your honor grip,
Let that aye be your border:
In slightest touches, instant pause —
Debar a' side pretenses;
And resolutely keep its laws,
Uncaring consequences.

"The great Creator to revere,
Must sure become the creature;
But still the preaching cant forbear,
And ev'n the rigid feature:
Yet ne'er with wits profane to range
Be complaisance extended;
And Atheist-laugh 's a poor exchange
For Deity offended!

"When ranting round in pleasure's ring,
Religion may be blinded;
Or if she gie a random sting,
It may be little minded;
But when on life we're tempest-driv'n,
A conscience but a canker —
A correspondence fix'd wi' Heav'n
Is sure a noble anchor.
. . . . . .

"In ploughman phrase, 'God send you speed,'
Still daily to grow wiser;
And may ye better reck the rede,
Than ever did th' Adviser."

Behind all the wretchedness of his life, and all the levity of his language, it is impossible not to see in that dark struggle the traces of the two main principles of Scottish religion which I have in these lectures endeavored to describe, and which, in one short, impressive passage, Burns has himself described for us: —

"Still there are two great pillars that bear us up, amid the wreck of misfortune and misery. The one is composed of the different modifications of a certain noble, stubborn something in man, known by the names of courage, fortitude, magnanimity. The other is made up of those feelings and sentiments, which, however the skeptic may deny them, or the enthusiastic disfigure them, are yet, I am convinced, original and component parts of the human soul; those *senses of the mind*, if I may be allowed the expression, which connect us with and link us to those awful obscure realities — an all-powerful, and equally beneficent God; and a world to come, beyond death and the grave. The first gives the nerve of combat, while a ray of hope beams on the field: the last pours the balm of comfort into the wounds which time can never cure.[1]

Walter Scott.

Of Walter Scott I have already indicated, by the many illustrations which his works supply, how he has sounded all the depths and shoals of Scottish ecclesiastical history — how entirely he has identified himself with every phase through which it has passed, even, it may be, those which were least congenial to himself. Episcopalian, and, in one sense, Jacobite as he was in his personal feelings, yet in his whole public life he never parted from the Church which as a Scotsman he claimed as his own. The worship of that Church was to him "our national worship";[2] its traditions and characters counterbalance many times over in his writings

[1] For the whole complex statement of Burns's life and teaching, see Carlyle's *Essays*, i. 324–398.

[2] Unpublished letter addressed to the Rev. Principal Baird, July, 1828, furnished by the kindness of Mr. Bailey.

those which he derived from the Episcopal communion.

It would require a separate lecture to point out the services which he has rendered to the Church of Great Britain as well as of Scotland, not only by the wholesome, manly, invigorating spirit of his works,— not only by the example of his untiring conscientious resolution, not only by the equity and elevation of his judgment of the contending factions in the Scottish Church and State, but by the firm yet tender grasp with which he handles so many of those graver questions which now, even more than when he lived, exercise modern thought. Such, for example, is the light which he throws by incident or argument, or passing speech, in one or other of his romances, on the due proportion of doctrine and practice; on the power of prayer; on the effect of miracles; on the intermingling of the natural and the preternatural in human history; on the relations of the clergy to the State and to the community at large; on the superiority of internal to external evidence; on the critical and philosophical comparison of the several parts of the Bible with each other; on the great controversy between authority and reason; on the relative advantages and disadvantages of the Roman and the Protestant Churches; on the distinctive peculiarities and the common features of the Churches of England and Scotland; on the historical characteristics of Christianity and of Mohammedanism; on the effect produced in all our views by the approach of Death and of Eternity; on the nature of true forgiveness; on the varying yet identical forms of superstition; on the essential difference between fanaticism and religion. The elucidations and illustrations which abound in those mighty works of fiction, of these and like problems, are more than enough to justify the place here given to him as one of the great religious teachers of Scottish Christendom. Happy that Church which has been blessed with such a theologian, whose voice can be heard by those whom no sermons ever reach, proclaiming lessons which no preacher or divine can afford to despise or to neglect.

Warning against the infallibility of parties.

In thus gathering up the fruits of the true spiritual Church of Scotland, I have dwelt on these individual instances partly because they bring out in a stronger light what I wish to express; partly also because they tend to enforce a lesson which, greatly needed everywhere at this time, is specially needed in the ecclesiastical atmosphere of Scotland. It is said that Oliver Cromwell, when addressing the General Assembly of the Church of Scotland, said: "I beseech you, my beloved brethren—I beseech you in the bowels of Christ, to *believe that you may be mistaken.*" It was a remark pregnant with wisdom, and equally applicable to Pope, Prelate, and Presbyter; and that was a true echo of it which was heard in the advice delivered by the greatest modern Scottish philosopher to the Seceders of 1843, and which is equally applicable to all phases of popular panic and contagious excitement, "*Be not martyrs by mistake.*" But over and above the general lesson which every son of Adam needs against believing in his own infallibility, I venture to think that there was a peculiar truth in the saying both of the Protector and the philosopher. It is this: that large bodies of men, especially large parties of men, not only may be mistaken, but are, by the very reason of their moving in masses and parties, likely to be mistaken. And this tendency to adopt party watchwords as oracles, and to turn all questions into party watchwords, is a peculiar temptation in our own time, and judging from past and present experience, has always been a special temptation in Scotland. Against this tendency one of the greatest safeguards is the contemplation of such individual examples as I have given, which strike across these superficial boundaries, and which prove the power of the individual being to stand by his own internal convictions, and to bring, if so be, the world round to himself, if only he is determined not to follow but to guide. Of all the earnest exhortations which Walter Scott delivered to those who were to follow him, the most earnest,[1] as though it were engrained in his mind by the long and bitter experience through which his own country had passed, is the entreaty to shun party spirit as one of the most fatal obstacles to the public good.

Whilst thus insisting on the elements of Scottish religious life, which are above and beyond all institutions and all parties, it is impossible to avoid the question (not what party, but) what institution most corresponds to these aspirations? And here we cannot doubt that, viewing it as a whole, and with all allowance for its short-comings, it must be that institution which alone bears on its front without note or comment, the title of "The Church of Scotland." Like all the other religious communities in the country it is compassed about with its own

The Established Church.

[1] *Tales of a Grandfather*, 3d series.

temporal surroundings; but it is the one which in its idea most answers to "the Church without a name," of which I spoke at the beginning of this lecture, the Spiritual or Invisible Church which owns no earthly head.

As of the Church of England, so of the Church of Scotland, and of every National Church, the glory is, according to the "golden maxim" of the "ever-memorable Hales," to carry, like the prophet Amphiaraus, a "blank shield with no device of sect or party." The Episcopal communion carries on its shield, by the mere force of its name, the device of Episcopacy. The "Free Church" claims by the assumption of that name the special device of the independence of the spiritual above the civil courts, or of the principle of the popular election of its ministers. The Cameronians exist in virtue of their ancient testimony for the Covenant. The United Presbyterians bear the device of the voluntary system and of the unlawfulness of contact with the State. But the Established Church, from which these have all seceded, bears no other device but the Thistle of the Scottish nation and the historic recollections of the Burning Bush of the Scottish Church. Whatever Scottish Christianity is prepared to become, that the Church of Scotland is prepared to be. It treats Presbyterianism, Episcopacy, Patronage, Non-intrusion, as in themselves mere accidents. It has gone through the various phases of the wild monastic clanship of the Culdees, of the Anglo-Norman hierarchy of St. Margaret, of the Scottish hierarchy of Robert Bruce, the mixed Presbyterian and Episcopal government under Queen Mary and James VI., the

Its historical character.

mixed Episcopal and Presbyterian government under Charles I. and Charles II., the purely Presbyterian government from William III. onwards. It has passed through the Liturgy and the Confession of John Knox, the Solemn League and Covenant, the Sum and Substance of Saving Doctrine, the Westminster Confession and the Westminster Directory; and, again, through the alternations of domination, from the Regent Murray to Andrew Melville, to Rutherford and the Covenanters, to Carstairs and the Moderates, to Chalmers and the "popular party." None of these phases need be altogether lost to it. The Westminster Confession, no less than the Solemn League and Covenant, will always be preserved amongst its historical documents, although both may have ceased to express the mind of the modern Church of Scotland; although, as time rolls on, the stern requirements of adhesion to the Confession which emanated from the Jerusalem Chamber be laid aside, as the far sterner adhesion to the Confession that emanated from Greyfriars' Church has been laid aside long ago. Its romance, its independence, its fervor, its prudence — must we not add its exquisite and unrivaled humor — these are the heir-looms of the Church of Scotland, which it has never lost, and which, whatever be the change of its internal form, it need never lose.

Its Presbyterian character.

There is yet this further merit which the Church of Scotland may claim. Whatever may be in store for its future, its past history and its present condition are standing proofs that not only Christian devotion, but Christian culture and civilization can coexist with a form of ecclesiastical government which dates only from the sixteenth century, and with a Confession of Faith which is derived not from Nicæa or Alexandria but from Westminster; not from Athanasius, or Constantine, or Charlemagne, or Thomas Aquinas, but Calvin. In the total collapse of the Episcopate through the larger part of the western world, since nine hundred bishops have accepted an acknowledged fable as an essential article of the Christian faith, every Episcopalian ought to be thankful for the existence of a living Christian Church, which shows that outside the pale of Prelacy Christian life and Christian truth can flourish and abound, even if it should fail amongst the Episcopal communions.

Its vitality.

And, again, it is a standing proof that the idea of a National Church, so fruitful in itself, so entwined with all that is noblest and best in the feelings both of citizens and of Christians, holds its ground against all the undermining influences brought to bear upon it. Nothing shows more clearly the inherent vitality of an Established Church, than that in Scotland it should have survived the tremendous shock of the Disruption. It is the glory of the Free Church that it maintained itself on the strength of a single abstract principle, by the sheer force of self-denying energy, and of a bold appeal to the scruples of conscience. It is the still greater glory of the Established Church that it maintained itself in spite of the loss of many of its most zealous ministers, by the strength of its ancient traditions, by its firm conviction of right, and by its promises of a glorious future; that it has received new life into its ranks, that it has had the courage to repent of its former errors,[1] that it has become the centre of hopes and aspirations unknown to its own former existence, or to the communions which have divided from it. The very word "Residuary" used against it as a reproach, was, and is, its best title of honor. Churches and secessions which build themselves on particular dogmas are not residuary; they gather to them many of the most ardent and energetic, but they gather also the fierce partisans and the narrow proselytizers, and they leave out of sight those who are unable or unwilling to follow the leaders of extremes. But churches which are founded on no such special principles, which have their reason of existence simply because they profess in its most general aspect the form of Christianity most suitable to the age or country in which they live, these are "residuary" churches, because they gather into themselves the residue of the nation, the simple, the poor, who are too little instructed to understand the grounds which separate the different churches; the refined, the thoughtful, who understand them too well to care about them, who care more for the religious, moral, and intellectual life of the people than for the Solemn League and Covenant, for Non-Intrusion, or for spiritual jurisdiction.

If, therefore, the liberal intelligence of Scotland can maintain its ground against the force of party spirit, there is little fear lest the Established Church of Scotland should lose its hold on the affections of the Scottish nation. To destroy it would not be to

1 As for example, the almost entire change of feeling in the Established Church with regard to the teaching of Dr. John M'Leod Campbell. See Lecture III.

destroy merely an ancient institution, with endowments which would be taken from it only to be uselessly squandered, and with opportunities for Christian beneficence which no wise man would willingly take away in an age where material progress is so disproportionately active — it would be to destroy, as far as human efforts can destroy, the special ideas of freedom, of growth, of comprehension which are avowedly repugnant to the very purpose of the Seceding Churches, but which are inherent in the very existence of a National Church.

Its relations to the Seceding Churches.

The Seceding Churches, whether Episcopal or Presbyterian, have doubtless their own peculiar missions. As in England, so in Scotland, it was the folly of the Established Church not to acknowledge and utilize these peculiar missions in times past, so it will be the wisdom of the Established Church in both countries to acknowledge and utilize them in times to come. One of the most distinguished of living Scotsmen once pointed out to me the striking architectural effect which presents itself on ascending to the old city of Edinburgh in the well-known view of the Hall of the General Assembly as seen through the vista of the Free Church college. Nowhere else is either seen to such advantage as when the chief institution of the Church of the Disruption forms the foreground of the chief seat of the Church of the Establishment. Take away either, and the effect would be annihilated. This is a parable which applies to Established Churches and Seceding Churches everywhere. The Mother Church, whether of England or Scotland, can only be properly appreciated when rising behind the foreground of the Dissenting Churches. The Dissenting Churches would lose half their significance if the Established Church, whose short-comings they desire to rectify, but from which they derive their original life, and which serves to them as a centre and support, were swept away. It was a miserable intolerance when the Established Church in ancient times endeavored to prevent the growth of Nonconforming communities that satisfied peculiar wants which from its very nature it could not equally supply. It would be an act of still more inexcusable barbarism if in our more enlightened age Seceding Churches were in their turn to insist on a new Act of Uniformity, and, by destroying the Established Church, extinguish aspirations which they can never satisfy, because they deny their lawfulness and condemn their development. But they can render to the Church and the nation of Scotland services peculiarly their own; they can, in times to come, as in times past, keep alive in the heart that peculiar fire of devotion and warmth which in Established Churches is sometimes apt to die out in the light of reason and the breath of free inquiry, just as the Established Church has been the means of sheltering the intelligence, without which devotion dwindles into fanaticism, and the charity and moderation, without which the most ardent zeal profits nothing.

For these and for a thousand like ministrations there is surely ample room without the necessity of diverting the energies either of the National Church or of its divided branches into the contemptible rivalry of destroying and crippling each other's usefulness.

Its claim for support from Englishmen.

The Church of Scotland has a claim on the attachment of all those who are unwilling to let go the opportunity of unfolding to the utmost the capacities of an institution which has already done so much for the civilization and the edification of the whole Empire. Englishmen and Scotsmen of all persuasions may well be proud of maintaining a Church which has at times in these islands been the chief support of the united interests of culture, freedom, and religion; a Church which Carstairs and Robertson, Chalmers and Irving adorned; which Sir Walter Scott and Sir William Hamilton supported, because they felt that no existing institution could equally supply its place; of which the leading statesman of the last generation, though an Englishman and an Episcopalian, thus spoke to the students of the University of Glasgow: "When I have joined in the public worship of your Church, think you that I have adverted to distinctions in point of form, to questions of Church government and Church discipline? No; but with a wish as hearty and as cordial as you can entertain, have I deprecated the day when men in authority or legislation should be ashamed or unwilling to support the National Church of Scotland."[1]

There spoke the true voice of the great days of English statesmanship. And no English Churchman who forecasts the signs of the times can fail to echo the hope. Doubtless the Church of England has much to suggest to the Church of Scotland which the Church of Scotland, at least in the present day,

[1] Speech of Sir Robert Peel at Glasgow. See Chalmers's *Life*, iv. 171.

is most eager to acknowledge. I yield to no man living in my hopes of the magnificent mission which is open to the Established Church of England, if only it be true to itself — if only it be convinced that the true method of self-defense is not merely to repel the attacks of its adversaries, but to turn its adversaries into friends by the fulfillment of its lofty vocation. But the Church of Scotland has also its own to give us in return. It gave us in ancient days one of the best of our prelates — the first complete model of a truly pastoral bishop, Gilbert Burnet. It has in these latter days given to us the Primate who most recalls the enlightened spirit of Tillotson — a Scotsman of the Scots — Archibald Campbell Tait. It has in these latter years set an example of noble liberality to all the Churches by its readiness in welcoming in its pulpits the ministrations[1] of Prelatists no less than of its own seceding members.

When I think of the cordial and intelligent sympathy which it has been my privilege to encounter in many a manse, east and west, highland and lowland; when I think of the freedom and charity which have inspired the ministrations of Greyfriars' Church in Edinburgh, past and present; when I reflect on the teaching that has gone forth and is going forth from the Cathedral and Barony Church of Glasgow, and from that noble University which has done so much in former days, and in our own, for uniting in the closest bonds of affection the intellectual and

[1] I am aware that the law of the various Presbyterian communions leaves it equally open to them to avail themselves of this liberty. But I believe that I am correct in saying that it is hitherto only in the Established Church that this liberty — at least as regards the Episcopal clergy — has been acted upon.

moral life of both countries; when I call to mind the true union of philosophy and religion which in the pulpit of the National Church welcomed the scientific gathering at Dundee; when I remember what I may be allowed to call my own St. Andrew's, with the genial intercourse and varied learning which has so often cheered my studies, as I have lingered there listening to "the two mighty voices" of its sounding sea and its vast cathedral: when I think of all these things, I cannot doubt of the true freedom and strength (in all that constitutes real freedom and strength) of the Established Church of Scotland.

It was, in old days, customary for Oxford divines to speak of the Church of England as Judah, and the Church of Scotland as Samaria.[1] That contemptuous thought has now been exchanged for a wiser and a better feeling. The most accomplished scholar, the most purely Oxford theologian amongst the Scottish bishops, has in these latter days spoken with a far truer and nobler sense of the mutual relations of the two Churches, and entreated them to be at one with another on the equal terms of "Euodias and Syntyche."[2] Yet Scotland might, if she chose, not altogether refuse the ancient reproach of Samaria. Samaria had prophets at times when Judah was in darkness. The stern Elijah, the beneficent Elisha, the simple Amos, the tender Hosea, had their home not in the southern but in the northern kingdom; and the hills and vales of Galilee nurtured the Divine Light which Jerusalem labored to extinguish. But there is, if I may continue the sacred parallel

1 See the *Lyra Apostolica.*

2 *Euodias and Syntyche,* by Charles Wordsworth, D. D. (Bishop of St. Andrew's).

yet further, a better and a nobler end for both. As in those two divided Churches of Palestine, so in these two once rival Churches of Britain, the highest prophetic instinct points to a time when these recriminations will cease forever, — "when Judah shall no longer vex Ephraim, and Ephraim shall no longer envy Judah."

CHRONOLOGY OF THE CHURCH OF SCOTLAND.

CELTIC CHURCH.

A. D.

360–432. St. Ninian in Galloway.
432. St. Palladius, St. Serf, and St. Ternan in Fifeshire.
454–601. St. Kentigern in Strathclyde.
563–597. St. Columba in Iona.
865. Migration of Kenneth to Scone.

MEDIÆVAL CHURCH.

1080. Marriage of Malcolm Canmore and Margaret at Dunfermline. Norman hierarchy.
1124–1153. Reign and religious foundations of St. David.
1305–1329. Reign of Robert the Bruce. Severance of the connection with England.
1440–1465. Kennedy, Bishop of St. Andrew's.
1472. St. Andrew's converted into a metropolitan see.

REFORMATION.

1539. Death of Patrick Hamilton.
1546. Death of George Wishart. Murder of Cardinal Beaton.
1547–1572. Preaching of John Knox.
1560. Adoption of the Confession of Knox, and abolition of the Roman Catholic Church by the Scottish Parliament, August 17–24. Meeting of the First General Assembly, December 20.
1561. Arrival of Queen Mary.
1565. Marriage with Darnley.
1566. Murder of Rizzio.
1567. Murder of Darnley.
1567–1570. Regency of Murray.
1570–1581. Regency of Morton.
1570. Restoration of Episcopacy.
1572. Death of Knox.
1574–1606. Preaching of Andrew Melville.
1582. Death of George Buchanan.

A. D.

1586. Death of Queen Mary.

1592. Restoration of Presbytery.

ECCLESIASTICAL STRUGGLES WITH ENGLAND.

1603. Accession of James VI. to the throne of Great Britain.

1606. Restoration of Episcopacy.

1618. The Five Articles of Perth.

1625. Accession of Charles I.

1633. Coronation at Holyrood. Valuation of tithes.

1637. Attempt to impose the English Liturgy. Tumult at St. Giles's.

1638. The National Covenant. General Assembly of Glasgow. Restoration of Presbytery.

1643. Solemn League and Covenant to enforce Presbytery throughout the kingdom. Assembly of Divines at Westminster.

1648. Westminster Confession of Faith. Longer and Shorter Catechisms.

1650. Battle of Dunbar.

1651. Coronation of Charles II. at Scone.

1660. Restoration.

1661. Rescissory Act. Death of Samuel Rutherford.

1662. Restoration of Episcopacy.

1665–1687. Persecution of the Covenanters.

1679. Murder of Archbishop Sharpe. Battle of Bothwell Brigg.

REVOLUTION SETTLEMENT.

1688. The Convention.

1689. Restoration of Presbytery.

1690. General Assembly. Separation of Cameronians.

1691. Suppression of Episcopacy.

1694. Carstairs and the Oath of Assurance.

1707. Act of Union.

1712. Patronage Act.

1715. Death of Carstairs.

1718–1722. "Marrow controversy."

1728–1729. "Simson controversy."

1734. Death of Wodrow.

1732–1734. Secession of the Erskines.

1736. Porteous mob, "Judicial Testimony."

1712. Legal Protection of the Episcopal communion.

1724–1727. Usagers and Collegers.

A. D.

1725–1739. Secession of the Glassites.

1741. First Preaching of Whitefield.

1744. "Leechman controversy."

1746. Division between Burghers and Antiburghers.

1751–1780. Administration of William Robertson.

1752. Secession of the "Relief."

1757. Tragedy of "Douglas."

1763. Hume and Campbell.

1779. Agitation on Penal Laws.

1780–1790. The Buchanites.

1798. Preaching of Rowland Hill.

1833. Deposition of Edward Irving.

1834. His death.

1843. Disruption.

1847. United Presbyterians. Death of Chalmers.

1745. Revolt of Charles Edward.

1746. Episcopalian Disabilities.

1765. Introduction of Scottish Communion Office.

1784. Concordat with Bishop Seabury of Connecticut.

1792. Repeal of Episcopalian Disabilities.

1804. Acceptance of the Thirty-nine Articles.

1838. Death of Bishop Jolly.

of the style shows an intimate acquaintance with the resources of the English tongue. The pleasant flow of the language makes the reading of the translation a constant enjoyment. We do not know the theory on which it is founded, or if it is founded on any theory at all; but it is certain that, apart from the nature of the topics under discussion, and the local coloring and environment of the scene, there is little to remind us that it is not an original production in the vernacular. For aught that is here indicated to the contrary, the bees that settled on Plato's lips might as well have swarmed from an English as an Attic hive.

* * * * * * * * * * * * * * *

The claims of Plato to the study and admiration of thoughtful inquirers in this age of experiment and analysis repose on his profound exposition of the ideas which lie beyond the domain of physical research, which no process of anatomy or chemistry can detect, and which are revealed only in the universal consciousness of humanity. No dissection of the brain, no tracing of the subtle threads of nervous action, no demonstration of the exquisite enginery of the heart, or the marvellous courses of the blood, throws the faintest light on the principle of justice. the sentiment of love, the obligations of duty, the aspirations of reverence, or, in one word, on the mystic Trinity of philosophy, the True, the Beautiful, and the Good. Of this sublime evangel, Plato was the consecrated apostle. His message still finds an echo in the soul of the ages. His words of "sweetness and light," of moral beauty and intellectual grace, so lovely in their transparent candor, so acute, and yet so gentle, so masterly in logic, and yet so tender in emotion, will never lose their significance and power, until sensation has taken the place of ideas in the consciousness of man.

From Blackwood's Magazine.

This work by Professor Jowett is one of the most splendid and valuable gifts to Literature and Philosophy that have for a long time been offered. Its first or most obvious excellence is the perfect ease and grace of the translation, which is thoroughly English, and yet entirely exempt from any phrase or feature at variance with the Hellenic character. Very few translations, other than the Bible, read like an original: but this is one of them. It has other and more recondite excellences. It is the work, almost the life labor, we believe, of a profound scholar, a thoughtful moralist and metaphysician, and a most successful instructor of youth; and it is manifest that the complete success that has attended his execution of the task is itself the means of concealing the diligence, industry, and ability with which philological and interpretative difficulties must have been solved or overcome. It is a great matter, even for the best scholars, to possess such a guide and help in the study of the original; and to others, desirous of knowing thoroughly and appreciating worthily the wise thoughts and literary beauties of one of the greatest writers that ever lived, the boon is inestimable. The Introductions to the several Dialogues seem to be excellent, and are appropriately directed to explain the point of view which the great Greek philosopher occupied, and to point out the fact that his very errors—and we think some of these very great—arose out of his keen perception of evils which needed a remedy, but which, we believe, can only be remedied by higher influences than any that were within reach of a Pagan Philosophy.

Ralph Waldo Emerson's Estimate of Plato.

Of Plato I hesitate to speak, lest there should be no end. You find in him that which you have already found in Homer, now ripened into thought—the poet converted into a philosopher, with loftier strains of musical wisdom than Homer reached; as if Homer were the youth, and Plato the finished man; yet with no less security of bold and perfect song, when he cares to use it, and with some harp-strings fetched from a higher heaven. He contains the future, as he came out of the past. In Plato you explore modern Europe in its causes and seed—all that in thought which the history of Europe embodies or has yet to embody. The well-informed man finds himself anticipated. Plato is up with him too.

Nothing has escaped him. Every new crop in the fertile harvest of reform, every fresh suggestion of modern humanity is there. If the student wishes to see both sides, and justice done to the man of the world, pitiless exposure of pedants, and the supremacy of truth and the religious sentiment, he shall be contented also. Why should not young men be educated on this book? It would suffice for the tuition of the race—to test their understanding and to express their reason.

From the British Quarterly Review.

Professor Jowett has accomplished a great feat in giving to the world a complete English translation of Plato's "Dialogues;" for it certainly is no small matter to have placed Plato in the hands of all, conveyed in language divested, as far as possible, of mere technicalities and scholasticism, and put in a form equally accessible and alluring to average students of ancient or modern philosophy. And as this is a real benefit to non-classical readers, so the work itself is a real translation, in so far as nothing is intentionally omitted. We have the genuine Platonic dialogues in their integrity, without foot-note or comment, in the place of the excerpts or extracts which the nature of Mr. Grote's great work rendered necessary, and of the occasional and somewhat too frequent omissions of passages in Dr. Whewell's equally laudable, but, perhaps, not equally successful, endeavor to present Plato—in part, at least—in a popular form to the English reader. From the very nature of Plato's philosophy, which is to a considerable extent tentative and progressive, and which is constantly working out with variations the same leading ideas, it is essential to the English student to have the work complete. The *Republic*, of which an excellent version by Messrs. Davies and Vaughan has for some time been before the world, is to a considerable extent a *résumé* of Plato's earlier views—an epitome of Platonism, in fact; but a student may know the *Republic* fairly well, and yet have a vast deal to learn from such dialogues as the *Theætetus*, the *Philebus*, the *Parmenides*, the *Timæus*—all very difficult in their way; or from the more genial *Protagoras*, *Phædo*, and *Georgias;* or the more transcendental and imaginative *Phædrus* and *Symposium*, which last may be called the most fascinating and brilliant of the dialogues, excepting always the *Republic* itself.

Some of the minor, easier, and shorter dialogues, which fall within the range of average school reading—the *Apology*, the *Crito*, the *Menexenus*, the *Lysis*, the *Charmides*, the *Ion*—hardly touch the Socratic philosophy in its deeper sense; they are genial sketches of the idiosyncrasies of the wise old man, or deal with matters distinct from dialectics properly so called. Very little of Plato proper (so to speak) will be learnt from these alone. But the subtle reasonings of Plato, in some of his greater works, are sufficiently difficult to make even the best Greek scholars glad to have occasional recourse to studied English versions, on which they can with tolerable confidence rely.

From the New York Nation.

When we expressed a wish that some attempt might be made to popularize Plato for the benefit of American readers, we did not anticipate that an important step towards its fulfilment was so near. This book is, as Plato himself might have said, a veritable ἑρμαῖον, and we fondly trust that no important public library will long be without it. We wish we could add the time-honored expression about "no gentleman's library," but we much fear that some of our gentlemen will prefer a basket of champagne (the cost of the two commodities being about the same) to such a "possession for ever" as Professor Jowett's Plato.

The work is remarkable on two accounts. It is the only complete English version of Plato executed by a single translator. Of the two previous, one was commenced by Sydenham and finished by Taylor, while the other (in Bohn's "Classical Series") is the production of three different hands. This fact, which by itself would only prove the industry and perseverance of the writer, is complemented by his thirty years' experience and reputation, of which experience and reputation we cannot hesitate to pronounce the book worthy.

POPULAR AND STANDARD BOOKS

PUBLISHED BY

SCRIBNER, ARMSTRONG & CO.

(SUCCESSORS TO CHARLES SCRIBNER & CO.)

No. 654 Broadway, New York,

IN 1871.

BIBLE COMMENTARY (THE) Vol. I. The Pentateuch. 1 Vol. Royal 8vo, with occasional Illustrations.................................$5.00

CURTIUS, Prof. Dr. ERNST. The History of Greece. Vols I. & II. Cr. 8vo, per vol...$2.50

DE VERE, Prof. M. SCHELE. Americanisms. 1 vol., cr. 8vo, $3.00

ERCKMANN—CHATRIAN NOVELS (THE). Each 1 vol., 16mo. With Illustrations...cloth $1.00—paper 50c.

——————— The Blockade of Phalsburg.

——————— The Invasion of France in 1814.

FROUDE, J. A. History of England. *Popular Edition.* In twelve vols. 12mo. The Set...$15.00

——————— Short Studies on Great Subjects. Second Series. 1 vol. cr. 8vo...$2.50

HARLAND (MARION). Common Sense in the Household. 1 vol., 12mo...$1.75

HARRIS (Mrs. S. S.) Richard Vandermarck. 1 vol., 12mo., $1.50

HODGE, Dr. CHARLES. Systematic Theology. Vols. I. and II. 8vo. per vol...$4.50

ILLUSTRATED LIBRARY OF WONDERS (THE). First Series. In 20 vols. Each 1 vol. 16mo., per vol. $1.50 With numerous Illustrations. The Set in a neat case for.......................................$30.00

——————— Second Series. Each 1 vol, 12mo., with numerous Illustrations, per vol...$1.50

——————— ——— Mountain Adventures.

——————— ——— The Wonders of Water.

——————— ——— The Wonders of Vegetation.

ILLUSTRATED LIBRARY OF TRAVEL, EXPLORATION, AND ADVENTURE (THE). Edited by Bayard Taylor. Each 1 vol., 12mo. With numerous Illustrations. Per vol..............................$1.50

——————— Japan (with a Map).

——————— Wild Men and Wild Beasts.

JOWETT, Prof. B. The Dialogues of Plato. In four vols., cr. 8vo., $12.00

LANGE'S COMMENTARY. Edited by Dr. P. Schaff. Each 1 vol. 8vo., $5.00

——————— Jeremiah.

——————— John.

——————— Joshua, Judges, and Ruth.

MACDONALD (GEORGE). Wilfrid Cumbermede. 1 vol., 12mo. With 14 full page Illustrations..................................$1.75

MULLER, Prof. MAX. Chips from a German Workshop. Vol. III. 1 vol., cr. 8vo...$2.50

——————— Lectures on the Science of Religion. 1 vol. cr. 8vo...$2.00

PORTER, Pres. NOAH. Elements of Intellectual Philosophy. 1 vol. cr. 8vo...$3.00

——————— Books and Reading. *New Edition.* 1 vol. cr. 8vo..$2.00

TRENCH, R. C. English Past and Present. *Revised Edition.* 1 vol. 12mo...$1.25

UEBERWEG, (Prof.) History of Philosophy. Vol. I, 8vo.......$3.50

WOOD (Rev. J. G.) Insects at Home. Illustrated. 1 vol. 8vo......$5.00

These books sent post-paid by the publishers on receipt of the price.

www.ingramcontent.com/pod-product-compliance
Lightning Source LLC
LaVergne TN
LVHW050523100826
845148LV00002B/422

* 9 7 8 1 4 2 5 5 2 0 6 2 5 *